French - Norwegian

LEARNING FLASHCARDS

FOR BABIES TODDLERS

alligator

alligator

The alligator is having a party.

fourmi

maur

The ant is red.

ours

bjørn

The bear loves you.

abeille

bie

The bee is saying hello.

oiseau

fugl

The bird is flying.

papillon

sommerfugl

The butterfly is pretty.

chameau

kamel

The camel has a hump.

chat

katt

The cat is happy.

dinosaure

dinosaur

The dinosaur is laying eggs.

poulet

kylling

The chicken is dancing.

vache

ku

The cow has a bell.

cerf

hjort

The reindeer has a toy.

chien

hund

The dog has two floppy ears.

dauphin

delfin

The dolphin is swimming.

canard

and

The duck has a bow.

aigle

ørn

The eagle is looking for food.

l'éléphant

elefant

The elephant is sitting.

poisson

fisk

The fish is a clownfish.

libellule

øyenstikker

The dragonfly is blue.

renard

rev

The fox has a red nose.

grenouille

frosk

The frog is smiling.

girafe

sjiraff

The giraffe has a long neck.

chèvre

geit

The goat has a beard

ver de terre

mark

The worm is in the apple

poule

høne

The hen has chicks.

hippopotame

flodhest

The hippo is big.

cheval

hest

The horse is fast.

kangourou

kenguru

The kangaroo has a baby.

chaton

kattunge

The kitten is playing.

lion

løve

The lion has a mane.

homard

hummer

The lobster is red.

singe

ape

The monkey has a tail.

poulpe

blekksprut

The octopus has food.

hibou

ugle

The owls have big eyes.

panda

panda

The panda wears a diaper.

porc

gris

The pig is fat and pink.

chiot

valp

The dog is brown.

lapin

kanin

The rabbit has a carrot.

rat

rotte

The mouse is writing something.

crabe

krabbe

The crab has two pinchers.

requin

hai

The shark is scary.

mouton

sau

The sheep are very fluffy.

escargot

snegl

The snail is slow.

serpent

slange

The snake has poison.

araignée

edderkopp

The spider is purple.

écureuil

ekorn

The squirrel has a nut.

tigre

tiger

The tiger has a red bow.

tortue

skilpadde

The turtle has a shell.

loup

ulv

The wolf is smiling.

zèbre

sebra

The zebra is black and white.

dinde

tyrkia

The turkey has two legs.

coq

hane

The rooster will crow.

perroquet

papegøye

The parrot is colorful.

hérisson

pinnsvin

The hedgehog has apples.

pomme

eple

The apple has a leaf.

abricot

aprikos

The apricot is yellow.

avocat

avokado

The avocado has a nut.

banane

banan

The banana is yellow.

la mûre

bjørnebær

There are a lot of blackberries.

cassis

solbær

The blackcurrants are yummy.

myrtille

blåbær

The blueberries are sweet.

cerise

kirsebær

The cherries have a stem.

noix de coco

kokosnøtt

The coconuts have juice.

figues

fiken

The fig has seeds.

grain de raisin

drue

The grapes are purple.

pamplemousse

grapefrukt

The grapefruits are sour.

kiwi

kiwi

The kiwi is fresh.

citron

sitron

The lemons are yellow.

citron vert

lime

We have lots of lime.

litchi

litchi

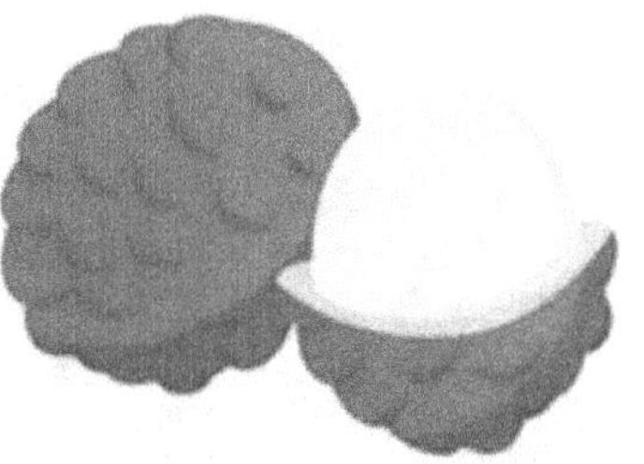

I like to eat lychee.

mandarine

mandarin appelsin

Oranges are refreshing.

mangue

mango

Mango is my favorite fruit.

orange

oransje

Mandarins are like oranges.

papaye

papaya

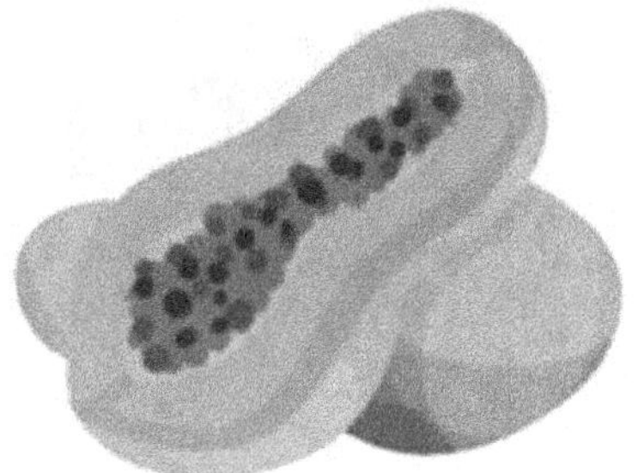

Papayas have lots of seeds.

pêche

fersken

Peaches are juicy.

poire

pære

Pears have a strange figure.

ananas

ananas

The pineapple has a thumbs up.

prune

plomme

Plums are healthy for you.

grenade

granateple

Pomegranates are all red.

framboise

bringebær

The raspberry is shiny.

fraise

jordbær

The strawberry has leaves on top.

pastèque

vannmelon

The watermelon is big.

mandarine

mandarin

The tangerine looks like an orange.

tarte

pai

I like to eat apple pie.

gâteau

kake

That cake is huge.

bonbons

sukkertøy

Candy is not good for your teeth.

biscuit

kjeks

Cookies are easy to make.

donut

smultring

I like strawberry donuts.

crème glacée

iskrem

The ice cream is melting.

muffin

muffin

The muffin has a cute wrapper.

pudding

pudding

We eat pudding on Christmas.

classeur

binder

I keep pictures in my binder.

livre

bok

I like to eat books.

sac à dos

ryggsekk

The backpack has lots of stuff.

les ciseaux

saks

I have scissors in my bag.

épingles

pins

Pins can hold stuff up.

agrafe

clip

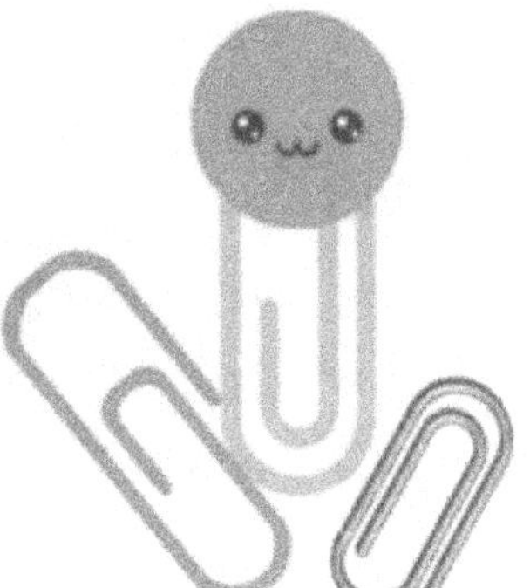

Clips can hold up paper.

papier

papir

I have lots of paper.

agrafeuse

stiftemaskin

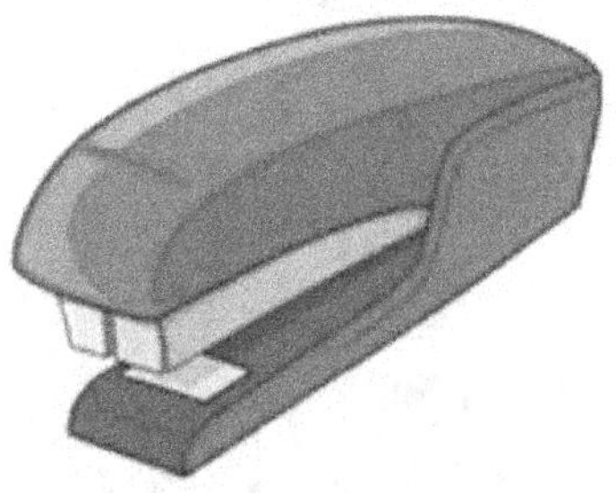

My stapler is shiny and red.

calculatrice

kalkulator

My calculator has buttons.

règle

hersker

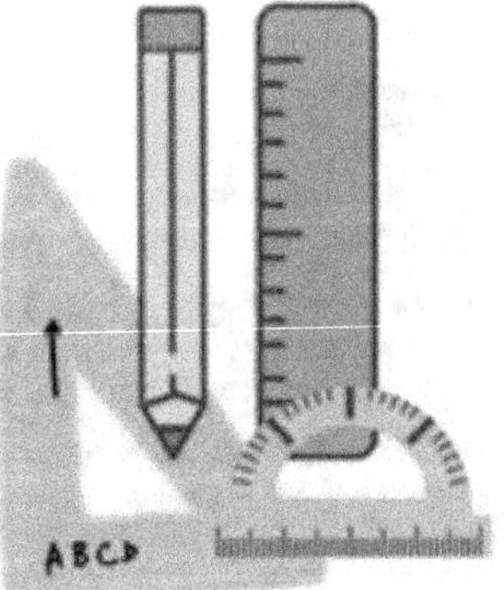

I have lots of rulers.

la colle

lim

The glue is sticky.

bibliothèque

bokhylle

My bookcase has lots of things.

calendrier

kalender

I have a calendar on my table.

chaise

stol

My chair is fancy.

l'horloge

klokke

The clock says that it's 3 o'clock.

ordinateur

datamaskin

I do things on my computer.

bureaux

skrivebord

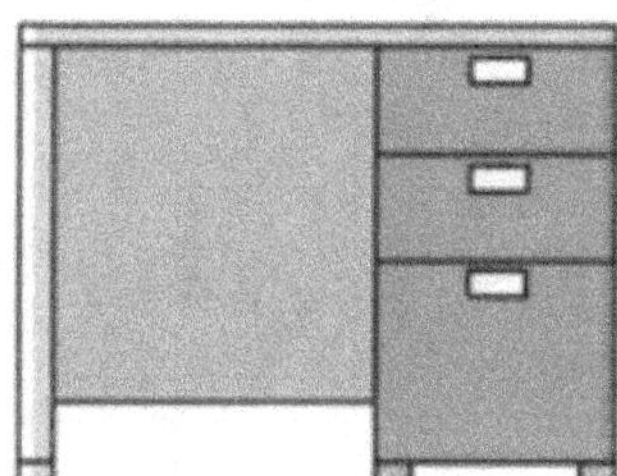

I put lots of things on my desk.

dictionnaire

ordbok

The dictionary has lots of words.

la gomme

viskelær

Erasers are used with pencils.

carte

kart

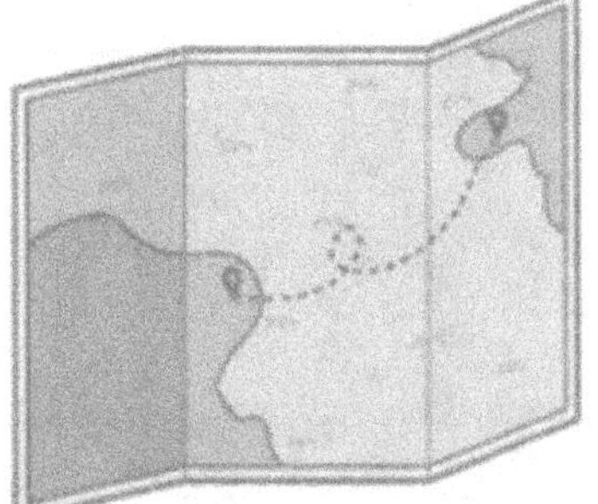

The map shows you different places.

carnet

notisbok

I use notebooks at school.

stylo

penn

My pen is very pretty.

crayon

blyant

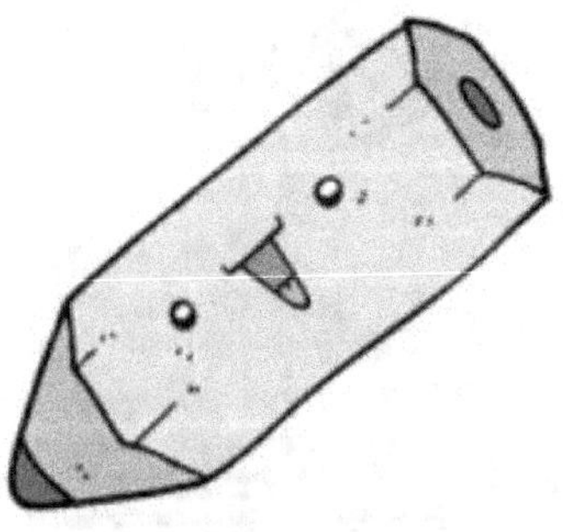

My friend gave me a pencil.

ceinture

belte

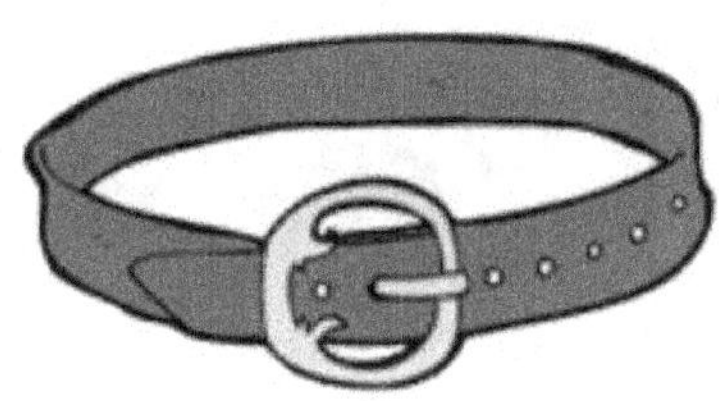

I have a belt on my pants.

bottes

støvler

I have big brown boots.

chapeau

hatt

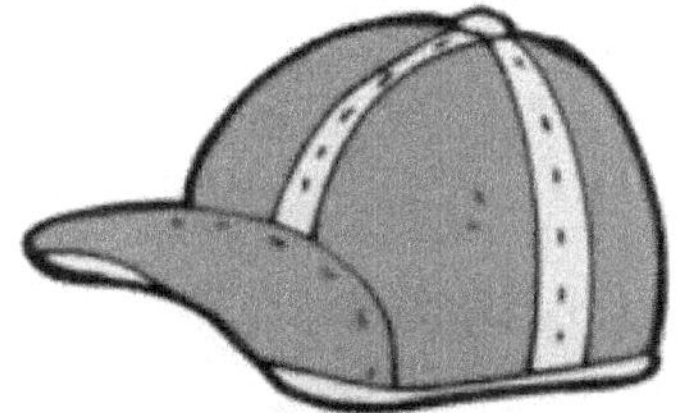

My mom bought me a new cap.

manteau

frakk

She has a long yellow coat.

robes

kjoler

My dress has a bow.

gants

hansker

I got new gloves.

chapeau

hatt

That hat is for a wicked witch.

veste

jakke

The jacket is cozy.

jeans

jeans

My jeans are long.

pyjamas

pyjamas

I sleep in my pajamas.

un pantalon

bukser

The bear is wearing pants.

imperméable

regnjakke

We wear our raincoats when it is raining.

écharpe

skjerf

The baby has a scarf around his neck.

chemise

skjorte

I like this shirt the best.

des chaussures

sko

I have red and blue shoes.

jupe

skjørt

My skirt has lots of buttons.

pantalon

bukser

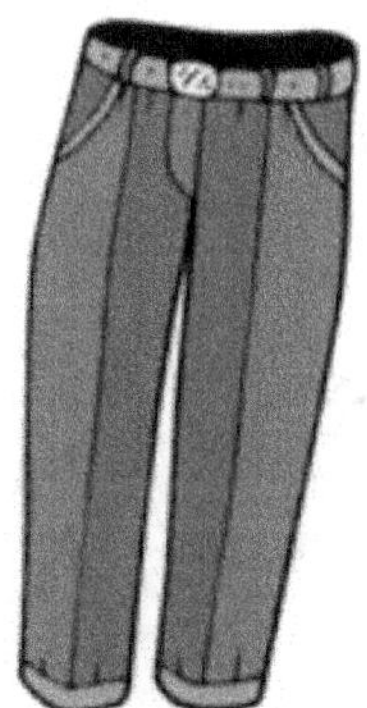

My dad wears slacks.

chaussons

tøfler

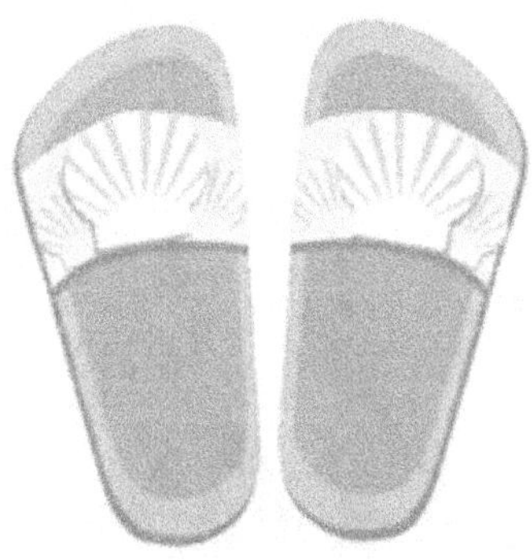

I have seashells on my sandals.

chaussettes

sokker

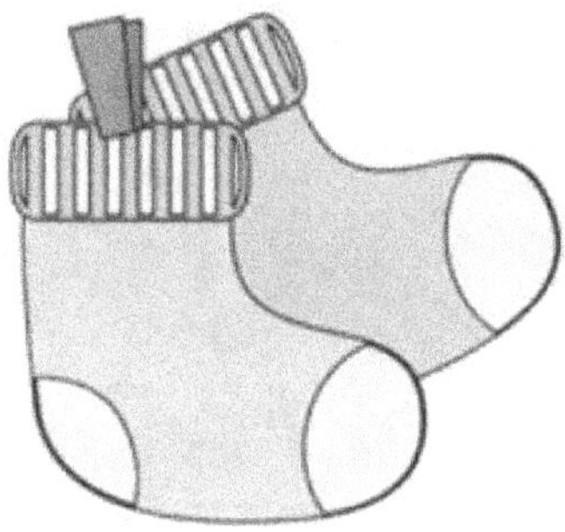

My baby sister wears socks.

costume

dress

My brother is wearing a suit.

chandail

genser

I am wearing a sweater for winter.

cravate

slips

My dad wears a tie to meetings.

pantalon

bukse

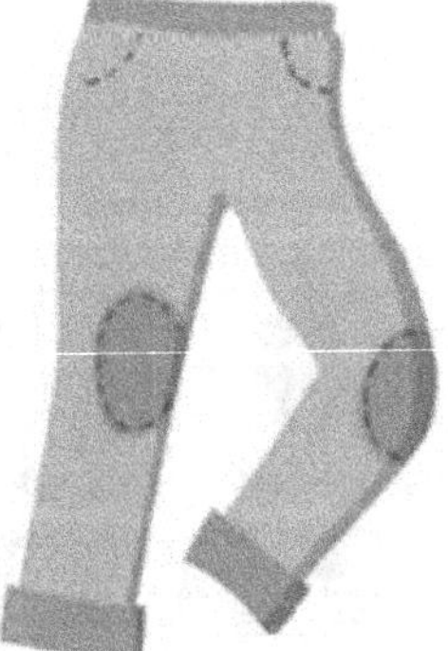

The trousers look like jeans.

slip

underbukser

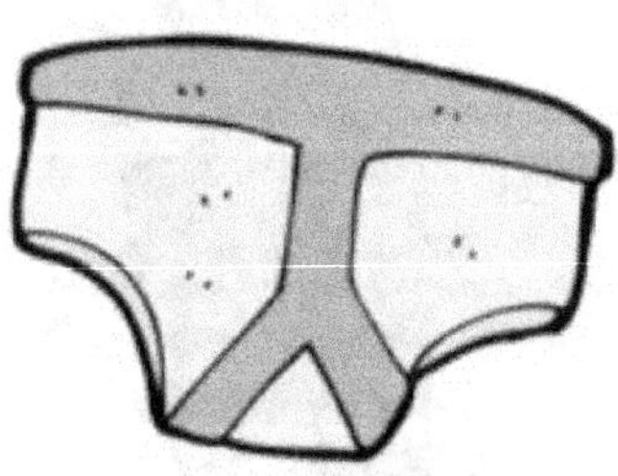

I always wear my underwear.

maillot de corps

trøye

My undershirt has a star.

une

en

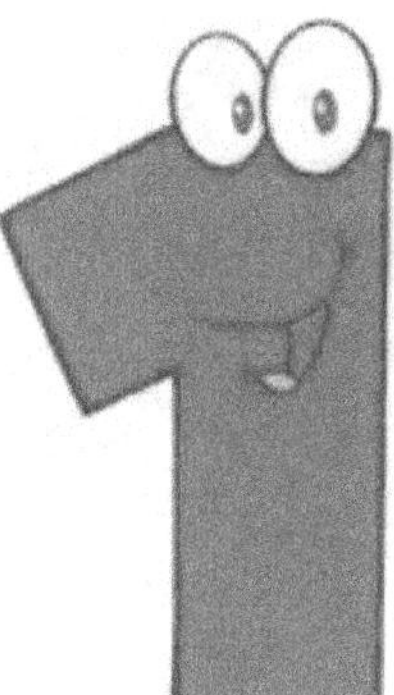

Number one and the bee are friends.

deux

to

The cat and the mouse both love two.

trois

tre

The bear gives number three a present.

quatre

fire

Number four is a home for the cat.

cinq

fem

Number five hatches an egg.

six

seks

Number six is going to eat a carrot.

sept

sju

Number seven is playing with the tiger.

huit

åtte

Number eight is funny.

neuf

ni

Number nine meets the parrot.

dix

ti

Number ten is smiling.

onze

elleve

Number eleven has big eyes.

douze

tolv

Number twelve is number one and two.

treize

tretten

Number thirteen is excited.

quatorze

fjorten

The number fourteen is vast.

quinze

femten

The number fifteen is green.

seize

seksten

Sixteen is my lucky number.

dix-sept

sytten

Number seventeen look alike.

dix-huit

atten

Number eighteen will go to the circus.

dix-neuf

nitten

I am nineteen now!

vingt

tjue

Number twenty has a zero.

fourmi

maur

The ant has lots of legs.

cloche

klokke

The bell will ring.

vache

ku

The cow has a bow.

poupée

dukke

She has a cute bear doll.

oeuf

egg

The chick has hatched out of the egg.

poisson

fisk

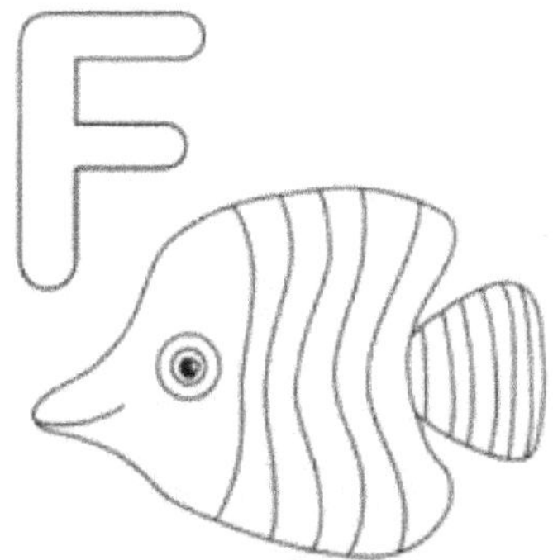

The fish is swimming in the water.

chèvre

geit

The goat is sitting on the grass.

chapeau

hatt

He is wearing a hat.

crème glacée

iskrem

I like to eat ice cream.

confiture

syltetøy

The kitten is sitting on the jam jar.

chaton

kattunge

The cat is sleeping on the floor.

lion

løve

The lion is waiting for the tiger.

rat

rotte

The mouse has lots of presents.

nez

nese

The reindeer has a red nose.

hibou

ugle

The owl is sleeping.

porc

gris

The pig will eat cupcakes.

reine

dronning

The queen has a big crown.

lapin

kanin

The rabbit is jumping up and down.

mouton

sau

The sheep have fluffy wool.

tortue

skilpadde

The turtle has a shell.

parapluie

paraply

The mouse is holding an umbrella.

van

varebil

The van is driving along the road.

pastèque

vannmelon

The watermelon has lots of seeds.

xylophone

xylofon

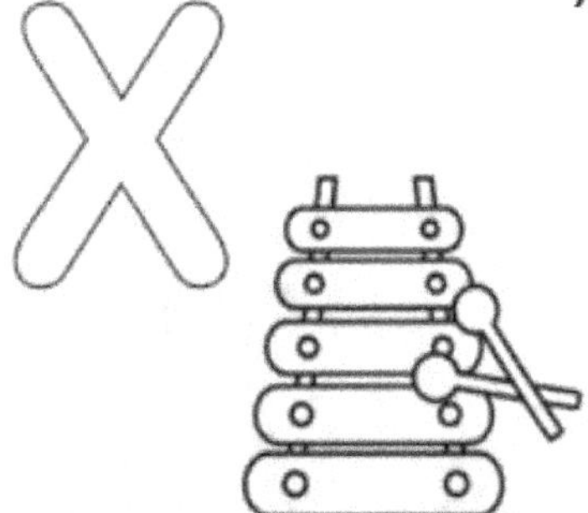

We are going to play the xylophone.

yaourt

yoghurt

We opened the yogurt can.

zèbre

sebra

The zebra is surprised.

rose

rosa

color the word and
the picture in pink

Most of my clothes are pink.

marron

brun

color the word and
the picture in pink

brown

My chocolate is brown.

gris

grå

color the word and
the picture in pink

gray

I don't like the color gray.

vert

grønn

color the word and
the picture in pink

green

The vegetables are green.

jaune

gul

color the word and
the picture in pink

yellow

Bananas are yellow.

blanc

hvit

color the word and
the picture in pink

white

The paper that I write on is white.

rouge

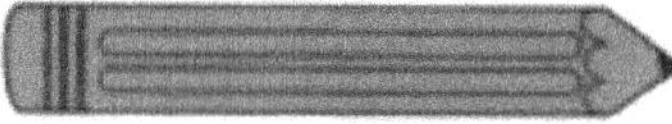

rød

color the word and
the picture in pink

red

Apples are red.

bleu

blå

color the word and
the picture in pink

The night sky is blue.

percer

bore

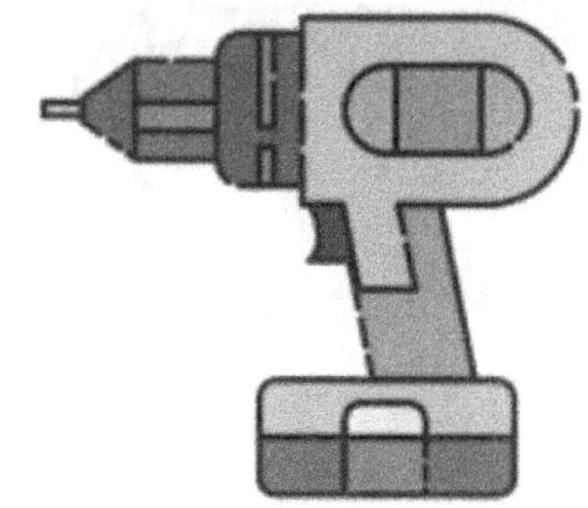

The drill will help us fix this.

marteau

hammer

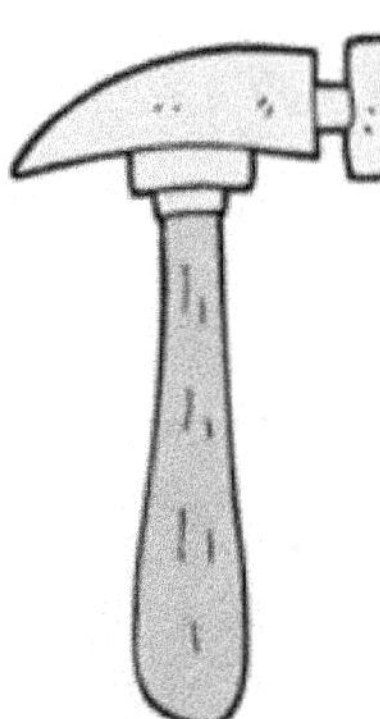

The hammer is going to nail the
picture.

couteau

kniv

The knife is sharp.

pinces

tang

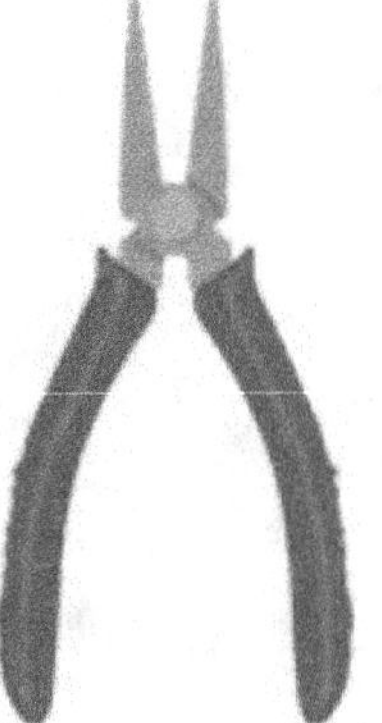

The plier is used for many things.

vu

sag

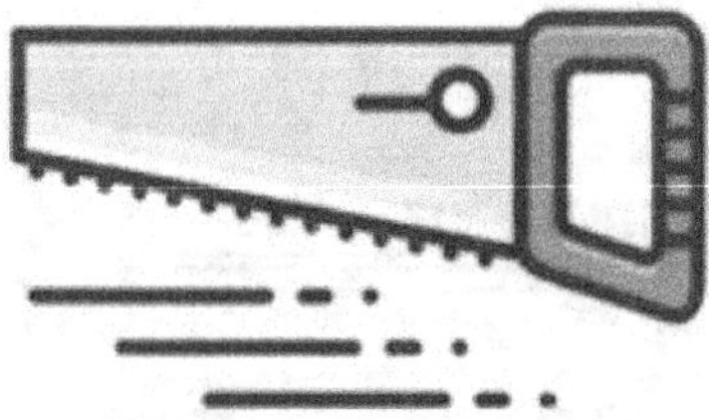

The saw can chop wood.

les ciseaux

saks

I use scissors to cut paper.

tournevis

skrujern

The screwdriver can screw in the knots.

clé

skiftenøkkel

The wrench can help unscrew the knots.

avion

fly

The airplane is going to leave now.

vélo

sykkel

The bicycle is beautiful.

bateau

båt

The boat is floating on the water.

autobus

buss

The bus is going to school.

voiture

bil

The car is green.

hélicoptère

helikopter

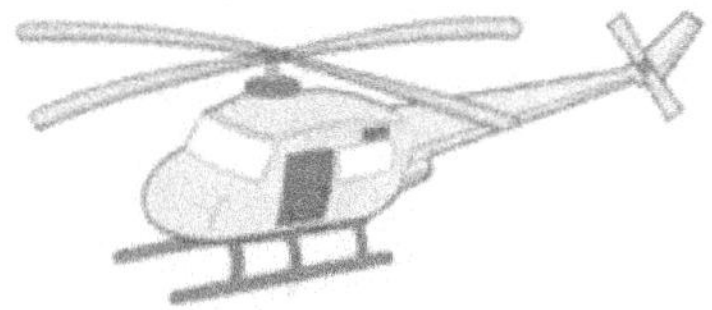

The helicopter is looking for something.

cheval

hest

You can ride the horse.

jet

jetfly

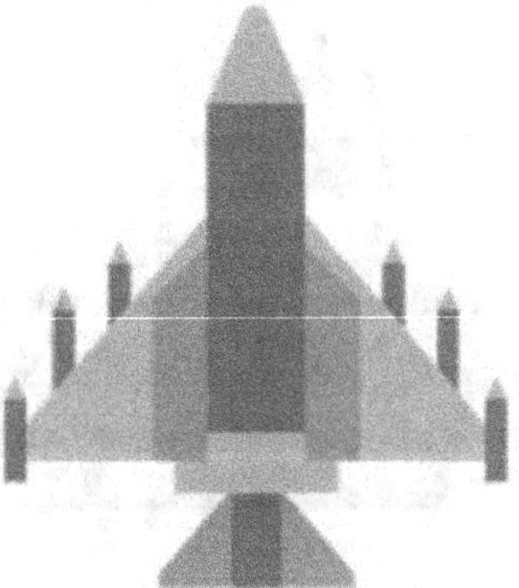

The jet is high-speed.

moto

motorsykkel

The motorcycle is on the road.

navire

skip

The ship is on the water.

métro

t-bane

My mom goes on the subway to work.

taxi

taxi

The taxi has someone inside.

train

tog

The train is going slowly.

un camion

lastebil

The truck has stuff in it.

asperges

asparges

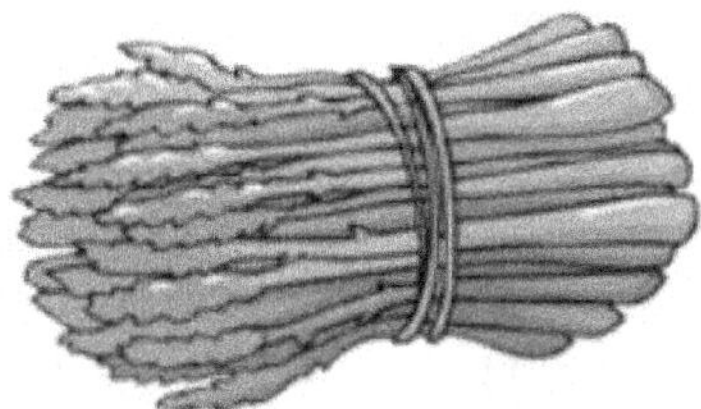

The asparagus is in a bundle.

des haricots

bønner

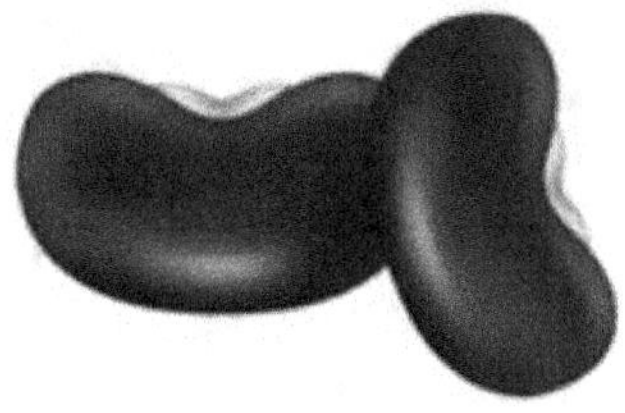

The beans are smooth.

brocoli

brokkoli

The broccoli is dancing.

chou

kål

Bunnies like to eat cabbage.

carotte

gulrot

The carrots are very long.

céleri

selleri

The celery has lots of leaves.

blé

korn

Corn soup is delicious.

concombre

agurk

The cucumbers are cut into pieces.

aubergine

aubergine

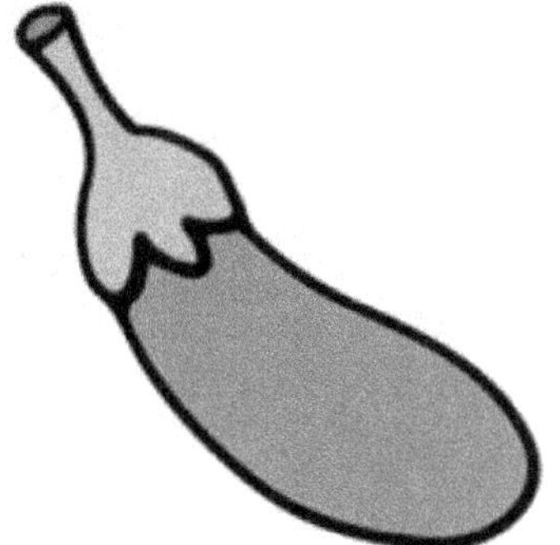

The eggplant is purple.

poivre vert

grønn pepper

The green pepper is juicy.

salade

salat

The lettuce is all green.

oignon

løk

The onions make my eyes water.

pois

erter

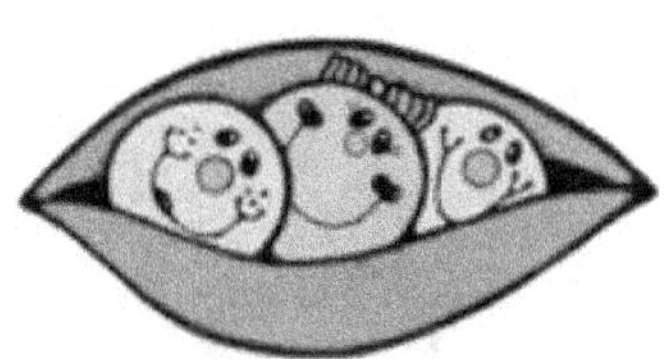

The peas are all in a pod.

patate

potet

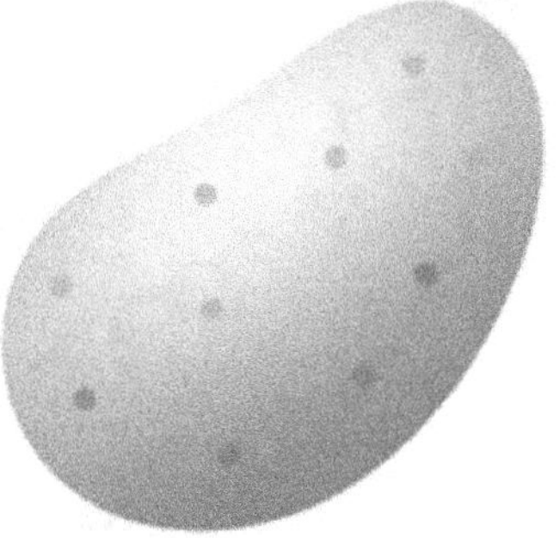

The potato is very shiny.

citrouille

gresskar

The pumpkin is for Halloween.

un radis

reddik

The radish is a type of vegetable.

épinard

spinat

The spinach is good with cheese.

patate douce

søtpotet

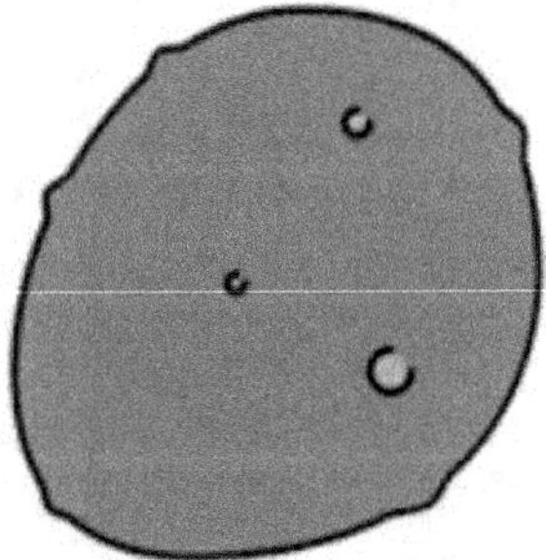

The sweet potato is quite sweet.

tomate

tomat

I don't like to eat tomatoes.

navet

turnips

My mom bought some turnips.

nuageux

skyet

The weather is cloudy today.

du froid

kald

I like cold weather.

cool

kul

The temperature is cold today.

brumeux

tåkete

The fog is so strong I can't see the city.

chaud

varmt

The fire is burning hot.

humide

fuktig

It's so humid and wet today.

pluvieux

regn

It's raining very hard.

neigeux

snowy

Welcome to snow land!

orageux

storm-

I hate the stormy weather.

ensoleillé

solfylt

The sun is shining!

chaud

varm

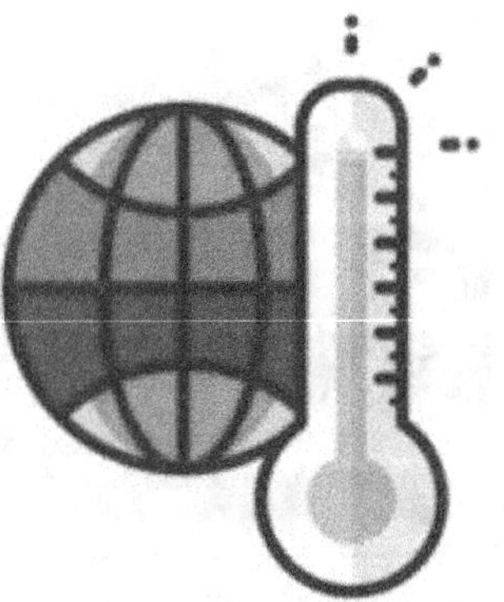

The whole world is warm today!

venteux

windy

The leaves are blowing away since it's so windy!

tante

tante

My aunt is very nice to me.

frère

bror

My brother is very fun to play with.

cousin

fetter

I love going to the playground with my cousin.

fille

datter

I like to read books with my daughter.

père

far

My father is playing with me.

petite fille

barnebarn

My granddaughter has blond hair.

grand-mère

mormor

My grandmother is very old and has glasses.

petit fils

barnebarn

My grandson and I are very excited today!

mère

mor

My mother likes to pick me up.

neveu

nevø

My father's nephew is my cousin.

nièce

niese

My niece is very good at playing ball.

sœur

søster

My sister is so pretty!

fils

sønn

My son likes to play with toy cars.

belle fille

stedatter

My stepdaughter likes the color orange.

belle-mère

stemor

My stepmother is pretty.

beau-fils

stesønn

This is my stepson, Greg.

oncle

onkel

My uncle tells lots of funny jokes.

bol

bolle

The bowl has nothing inside.

tasse

kopp

My mom drinks her coffee out of a cup.

plat

tallerken

That dish has a bone inside.

fourchette

gaffel

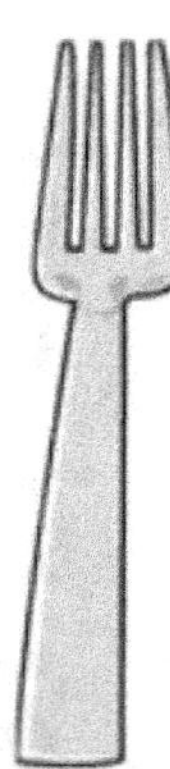

We have more spoons than forks.

verre

glass

I have a glass of water on my desk.

couteau

kniv

I have a knife in my kitchen.

agresser

krus

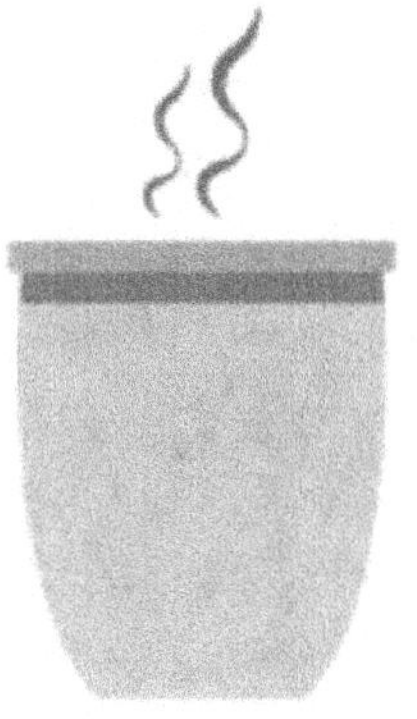

This mug of coffee is for my dad.

serviette de table

serviett

You can use the napkins to clean your hands.

poivre

pepper

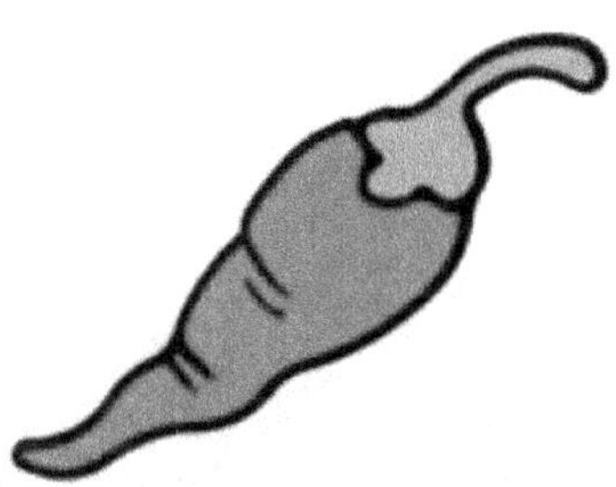

The pepper is very spicy.

lanceur

kaster

Pour yourself some lemonade from the pitcher.

assiette

tallerken

Can you help me wash the plates?

salade

salat

The salad is very healthy for you.

sel

salt

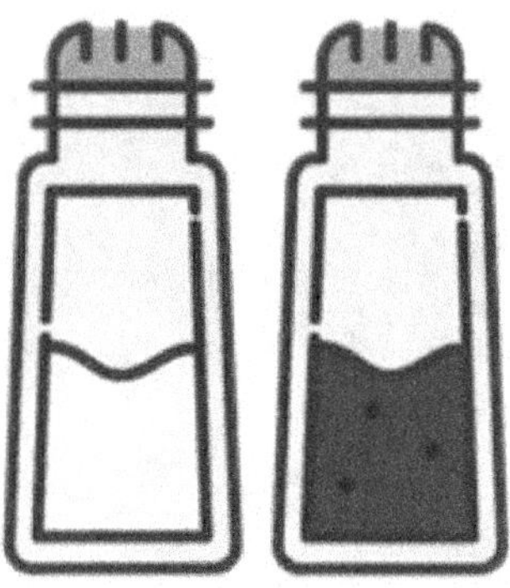

The salt tastes good with a few pinches of pepper.

soucoupe

tallerken

The plate is for my cup.

cuillère

skje

I use a spoon to eat my rice.

sucre

sukker

The pack of sugar is very heavy.

dimanche

søndag

Sunday

Sunday is the day to go to Church!

lundi

mandag

Monday

Monday is the day to start school.

mardi

tirsdag

Tuesday

We will go to the shops on Tuesday.

mercredi

onsdag

Wednesday

Wednesday is hard to spell!

jeudi

torsdag

Thursday

Thursday is the fourth day of the week!

vendredi

fredag

Friday

My birthday is on Friday!

samedi

lørdag

Saturday

Saturday is the weekend!

cuire

bake

The chef will bake a cake.

ébullition

kok opp

I will boil the eggs.

griller

broil

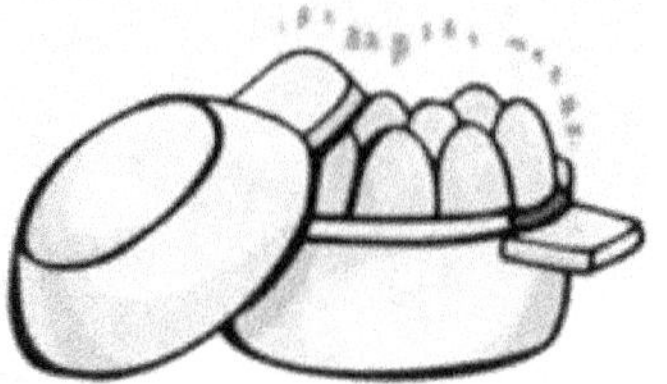

Broil is very yummy.

ouvre-boîte

boks åpner

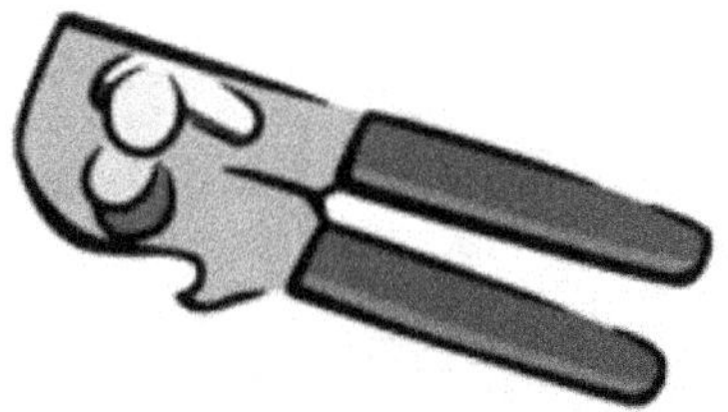

That can opener is used for opening cans.

frire

steke

The pan can fry lots of things.

gril

grille

We have a grill in our backyard.

tasse à mesurer

desilitermål

My mom uses the measuring cup for baking.

cuillère à mesurer

måleskje

I use a measuring spoon to eat my dessert.

four micro onde

mikrobølgeovn

The microwave is used to heat food.

bol à mélanger

miksebolle

She is using the mixing bowl to mix things.

serviettes en papier

tørkepapir

Dry your hands with paper towels.

poché aux œufs

egg poach

The poach is put on noodles.

porte pot

potte holder

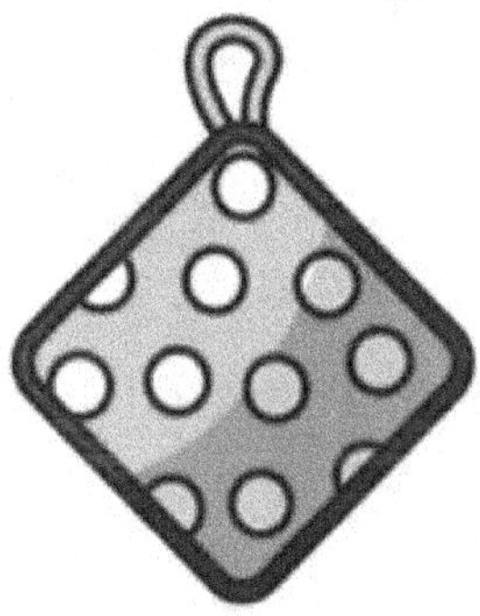

The potholder is soft.

rôti

steke

The chef made roast chicken.

rouleau à pâtisserie

kjevle

He is holding a rolling pin.

brouiller

scramble

My mom is making scrambled eggs for breakfast.

mijoter

småkoke

The simmer is rice today.

couteau

kniv

The knife is sharp.

cuillère

skje

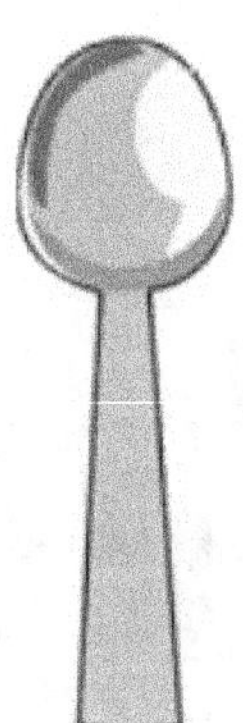

I eat my food with a spoon and fork.

spatule

stekespade

The spatula will help us flip the steak over.

vapeur

damp

The steam is coming from the pot.

passoire

sil

The strainer is used to strain stuff.

minuteur

tidsur

I set my timer for 12:00.

fourchette

gaffel

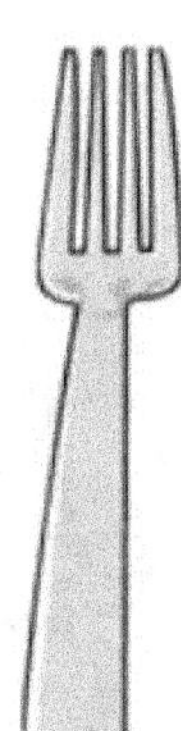

I have lots of metallic forks.

grille-pain

brødrister

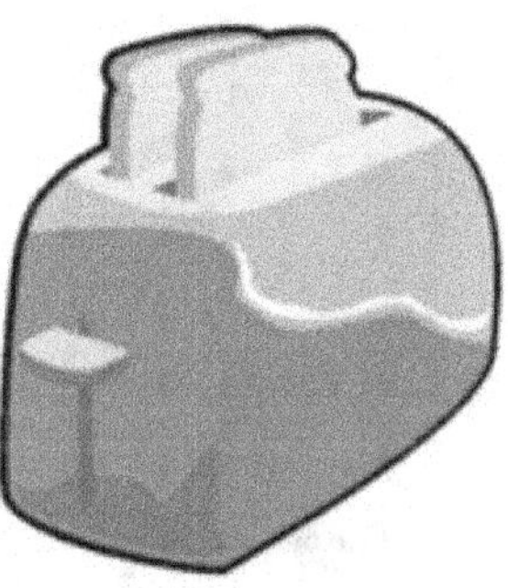

The toaster will toast my bread.

bouilloire

kjele

The kettle has tea inside.

réfrigérateur

kjøleskap

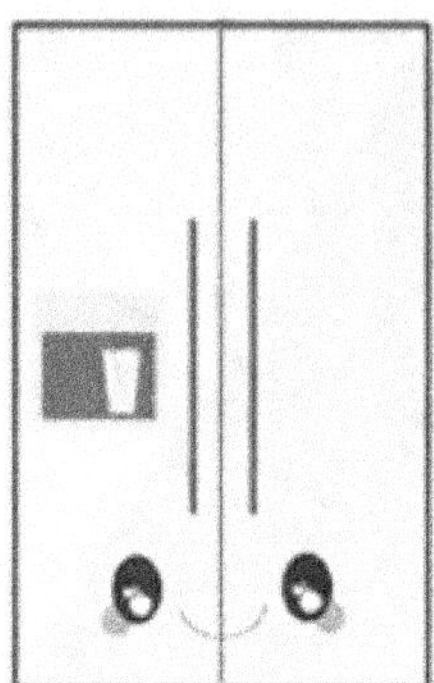

The refrigerator has lots of things inside.

mixeur

blender

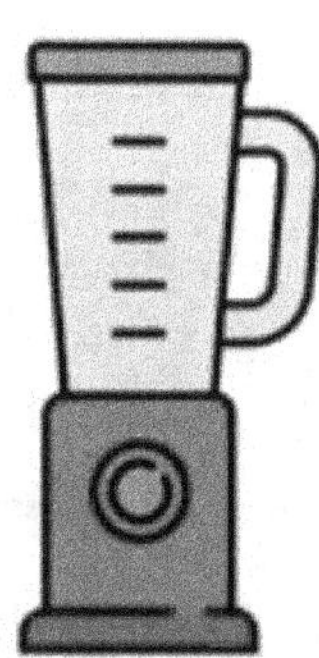

The blender will mix up my fruits.

cabinets

skap

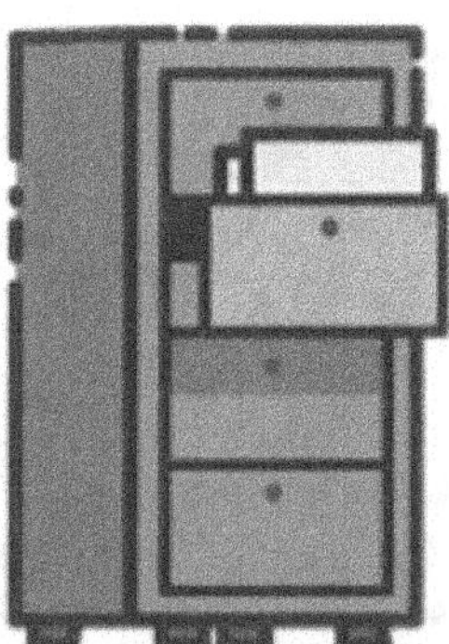

The cabinet has my paper inside.

placard

skap

The cupboard has lots of books.

four micro onde

mikrobølgeovn

The microwave will heat my food.

arrière

tilbake

She has a slender back.

des joues

kinn

She kisses her mom on the cheek.

poitrine

bryst

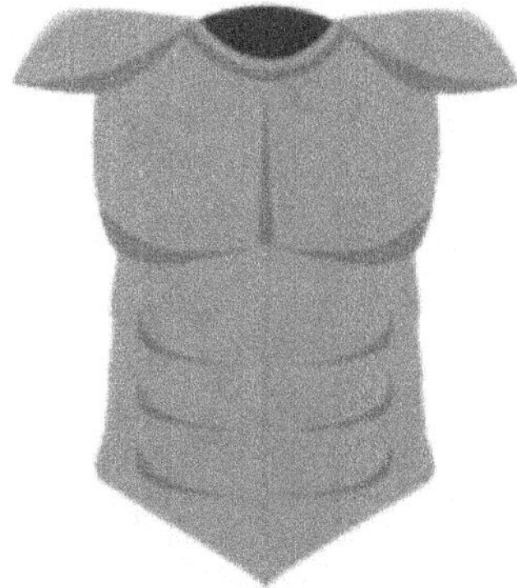

The armor is for your chest.

menton

hake

This is my chin!

oreilles

ører

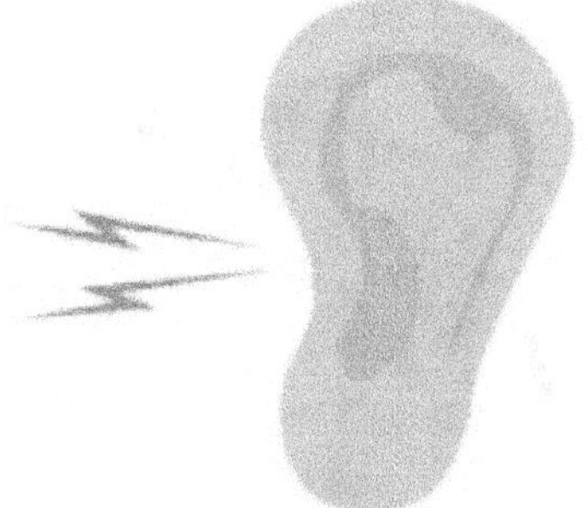

The ear is hearing something.

les sourcils

øyenbrynene

The eyebrows are raised.

yeux

øyne

The eyes are blue.

pieds

føtter

I have one pair of feet.

des doigts

fingre

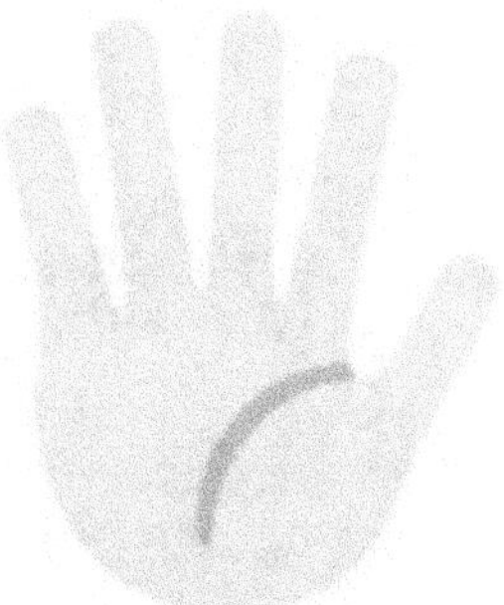

The fingers are waving at us.

pied

fot

My foot has five fingers.

front

panne

My brain is behind my forehead.

cheveux

hår

My hair is long and black.

# mains hender 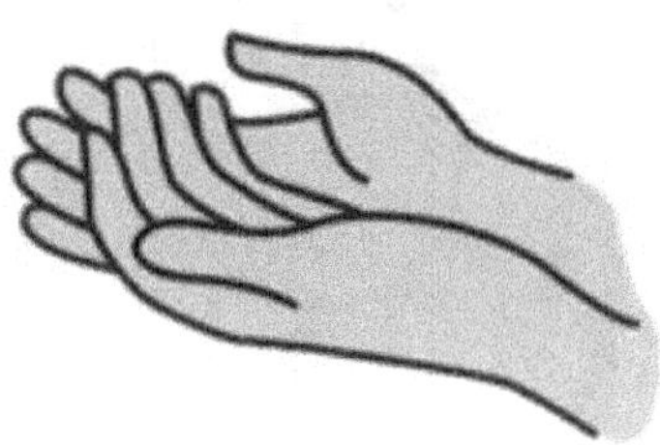 I will wash my hands in the sink.	# tête hode  She has a big head.
# les hanches hofter  The gorilla has his hands on his hips.	# les genoux knær  She is begging on her knees.
# jambes ben  The tiger has strong legs.	# lèvres lepper 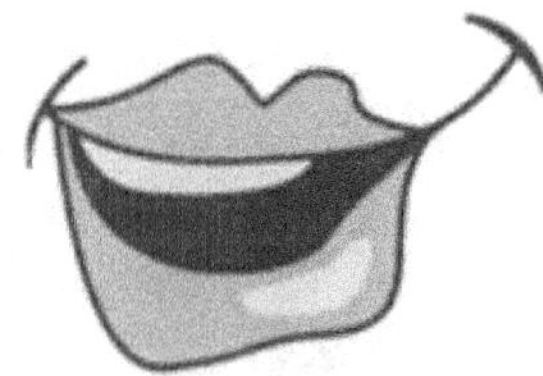 The lips have lipstick on.

bouche

munn

He is covering his mouth with his hand.

cou

nakke

The necklace is very special to me.

nez

nese

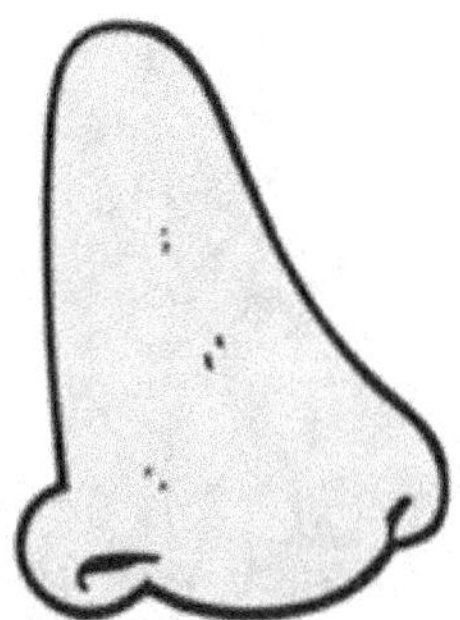

The nose smells something.

épaules

skuldre

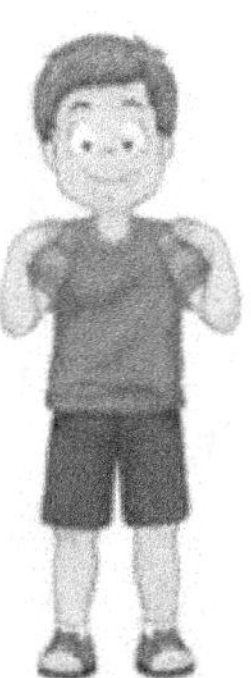

He puts his hands on his shoulders.

estomac

mage

He has a big stomach.

les dents

tenner

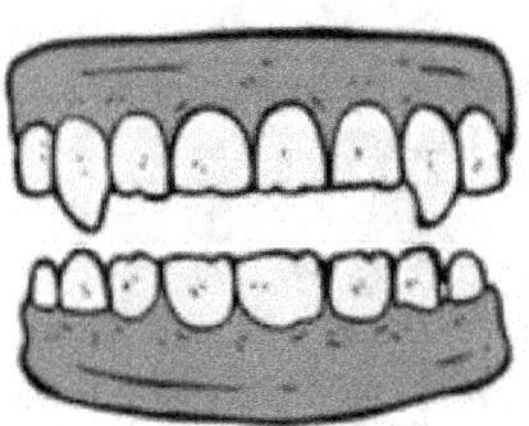

The teeth are clean and white.

gorge

hals

He has a sore throat today.

les orteils

tær

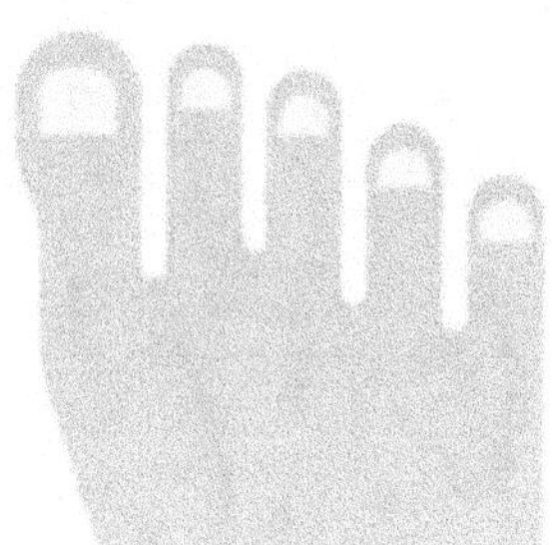

My toes are small.

langue

tunge

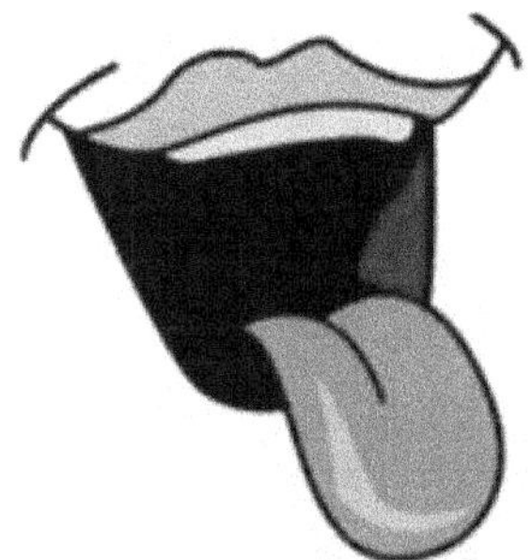

My tongue is licking ice cream.

dent

tann

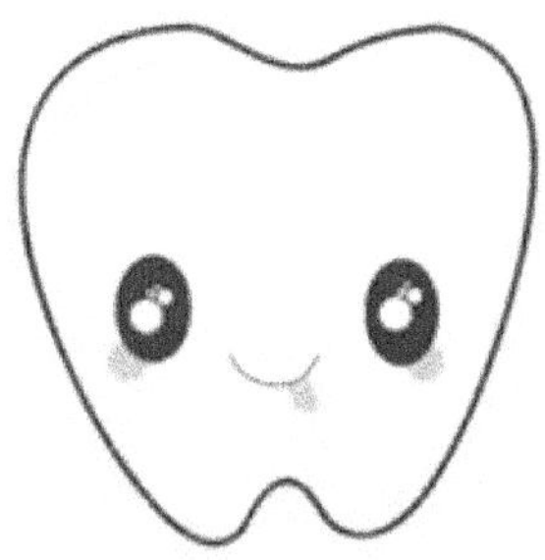

The tooth has big eyes.

taille

midje

He has his hands on his waist.

salopette

kjeledress

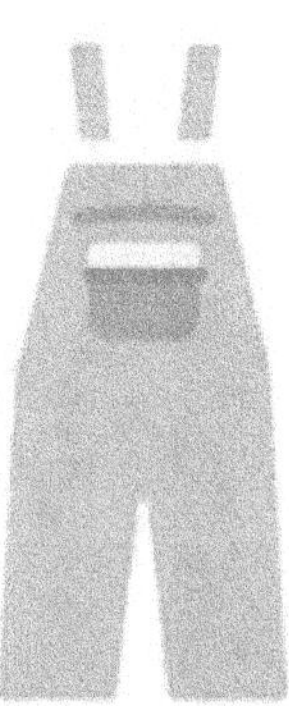

I bought these overalls for you!

mitaines

votter

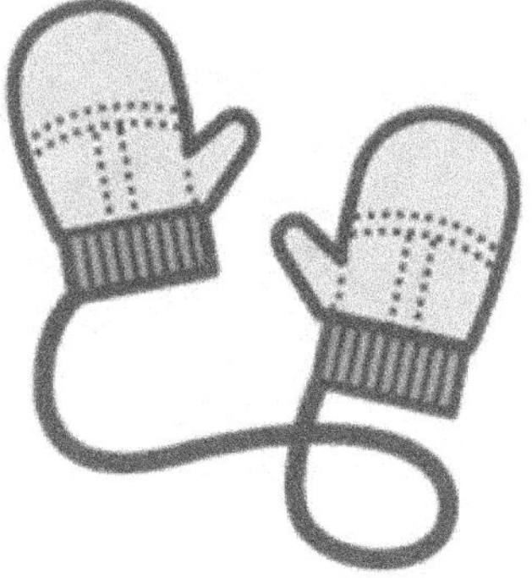

The mittens are very warm.

bonnet

beanie

The beanie is for winter.

tablier

forkle

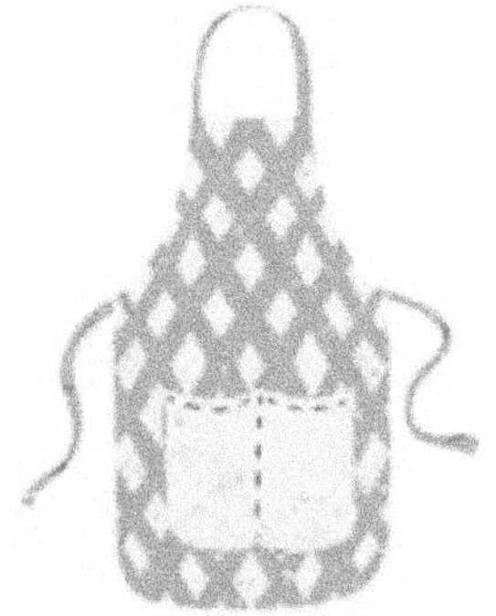

I wear my apron when I bake.

poupée

dukke

The doll is for my baby sister.

hochets

rangler

The rattle is for the baby.

jouet

leketøy

The toy is very fun.

couche

bleie

The baby has to wear a diaper.

berceau

bassinet

She is sleeping in her bassinet.

bavoir

smekke

My baby brother has to wear his
bib when he is eating.

octogone

octagon

The octagon is saying okay!

triangle

triangel

The triangle has three corners.

carré

torget

Square

The square has four sides.

cercle

sirkel

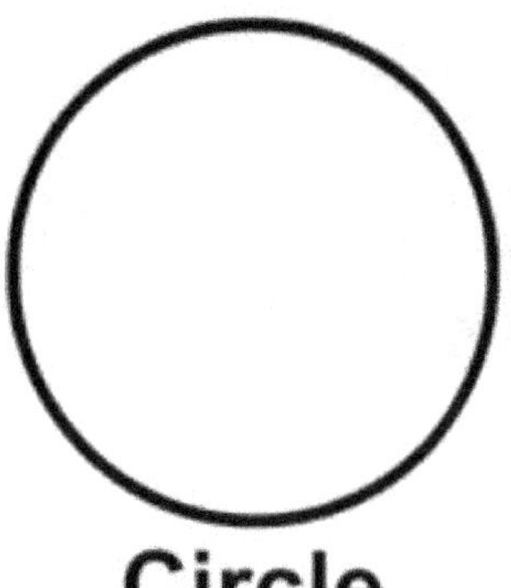

Circle

The circle is round.

ovale

oval

The oval shape looks like a circle.

cœur

hjerte

I drew a heart on my paper.

traverser

kryss

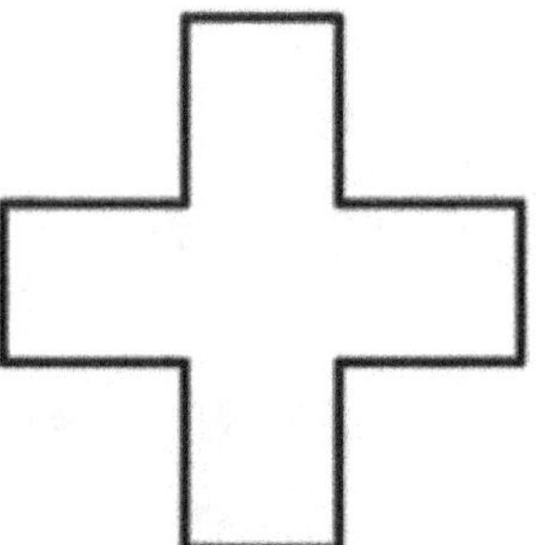

That sign is a cross.

la flèche

pil

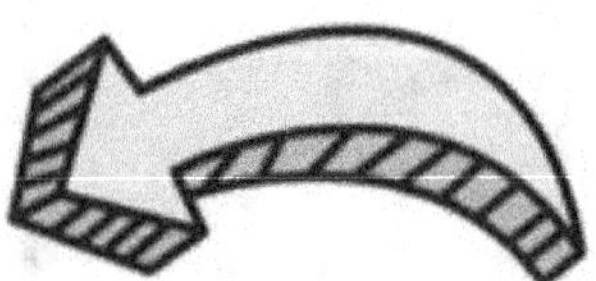

The arrow is pointing this way.

cube

cube

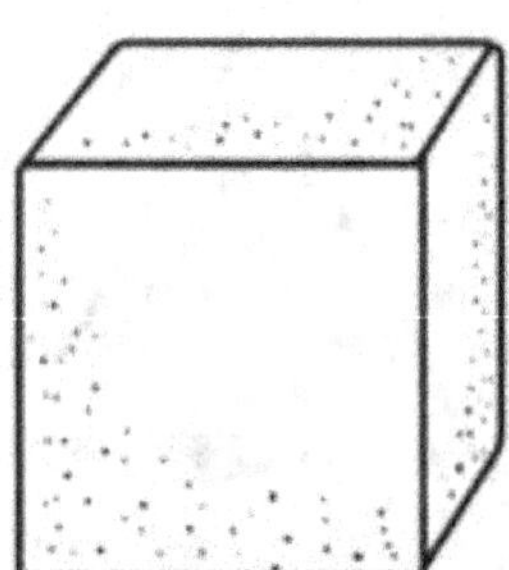

The cube is 3D.

étoile

stjerne

The star is yellow and shiny.

tir à l'arc

bueskyting

The archery is where you aim.

badminton

badminton

My favorite sport is badminton.

criquet

siriss

I am very good at cricket.

bowling

bowling

I got one pin down at bowling!

boxe

boksing

The boxing gloves are hot.

tennis

tennis

He can hit the ball in tennis.

faire de la planche a roulettes

rullebrettkjøring

He skateboards to school.

planche de surf

surfboarding

The shark loves surfing in the ocean.

le hockey

hockey

I like to play Ice hockey.

yoga

yoga

He is closing his eyes and doing yoga.

épée

sverdkamper

They are fencing and dueling together.

aptitude

fitness

She will do some fitness in the pool.

gymnastique

gymnastikk

He can do brilliant gymnastics.

karaté

karate

She is good at kicking in Karate.

volley-ball

volleyball

She is holding a volleyball.

musculation

vektløfting

The girl with brown hair can do weightlifting.

basketball

basketball

He can balance the ball with one finger in basketball.

base-ball

baseball

The little chick is in the finales at baseball.

le rugby

rugby

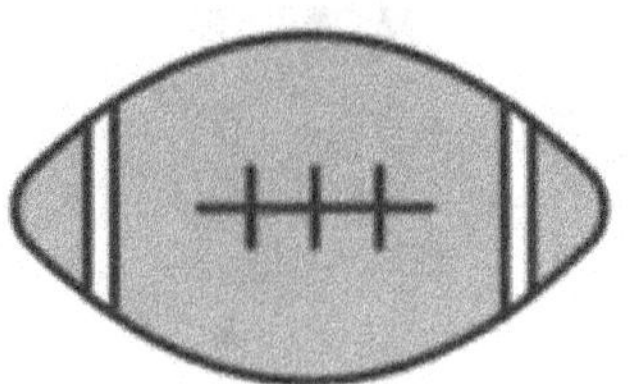

The rugby ball has white stripes.

lutte

bryting

The sumo will compete in wrestling.

course de voitures

billøp

He is number one for car racing.

cyclisme

sykling

He is peacefully cycling on the road.

fonctionnement

løping

He is running while listening to his earphones.

tennis de table

bordtennis

My brother and dad will play table tennis.

pêche

fiske

He will go to the river to fish.

judo

judo

She has a red belt in Judo.

escalade

klatring

He will climb the ladder.

tournage

skyting

He is shooting the archery board.

le golf

golf

She is going to compete in the golf competition.

balade

ri

He will ride his scooter.

asseyez-vous

sitt ned

They are sitting down together.

se lever

stå opp

She likes to stand up.

bats toi

slåss

They are fighting over the book.

rire

latter

He is laughing so hard!

lis

lese

She read a picture book.

jouer

spille

He went to play on the slide.

ecoutez

lytte

He listened for the ice cream cart.

pleurer

gråte

He cried because he got a bad grade.

pense

synes at

He thought that the test would be hard.

chanter

synge

He sang for the concert.

regarder la télévision

se på tv

He watched TV the whole night.

danse

danse

She was a good dancer.

allumer

slå på

The light is turned on.

éteindre

skru av

The light is turned off.

gagner

vinne

He won the contest.

mouche

fly

The parrot can fly.

couper

kutte opp

He was cutting his nails.

désinvolte

kast

He threw away the garbage.

dormir

sove

He slept soundly.

fermer

lukk

He closed his mouth shut.

ouvert

åpen

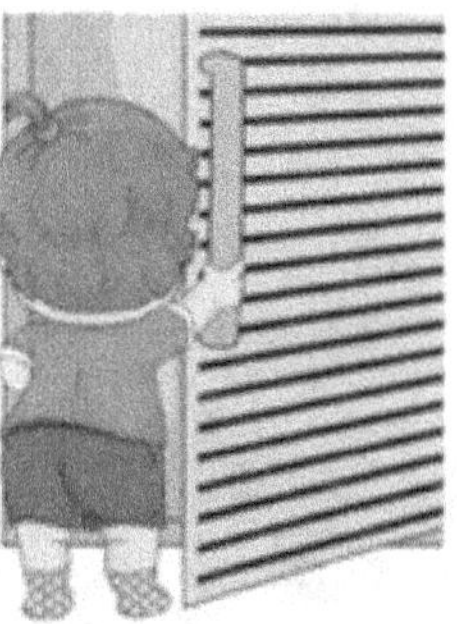

She opened the bathroom door.

écrire

skrive

She wrote with a pencil.

donner

gi

Santa gave her a present.

sauter

hoppe

She had fun jumping.

manger

spise

The shark ate yummy ice cream.

boisson

drikke

The old British man drank tea.

cuisinier

kokk

The microwave cooked his soup.

lavage

vask

You need to remember to wash your hands.

attendre

vente

He was waiting for the bus.

montée

klatre

She climbed a lot of mountains.

parler

snakke

Two best friends were talking together.

crawl

crawl

The baby crawled on the floor.

rêver

drøm

The Sloth dreamed about eating leaves.

creuser

grave

That strong man dug a swimming pool.

taper

klapp

The baby clapped her hands.

tricoter

strikke

She knits with the purple string.

coudre

sy

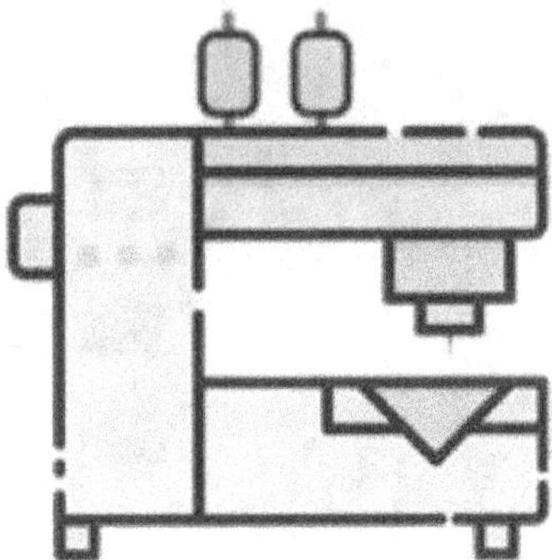

That is a sewing machine.

odeur

lukt

The perfume smelled great.

baiser

kysse

He kissed his mother.

étreinte

klem

They hugged each other.

ronfler

snorke

The tiger snored.

baigner

bade

He took a bath.

s'incliner

bukker

He bowed to the judge.

peindre

maling

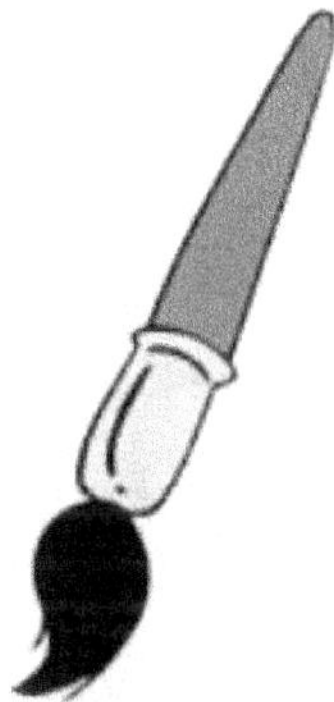

He painted a colorful picture.

se plonger

stupe

He dove to the deepest part of the ocean.

ski

ski

The ski was expensive.

empiler

stable

The books are stacked high.

acheter

kjøpe

They bought cereal.

secouer

riste

They shook hands together.

programmeur

programmerer

He was a smart computer programmer.

vétérinaire

veterinær

She is a veterinarian.

vendeur de rue

gate selger

That street vendor sells hot dogs.

mineur

gruvearbeider

That Miner will find gold.

prof

lærer

The owl is the teacher.

groom

bellboy

That Bellboy is fat.

orateur

høyttaler

The chicken is a great Speaker.

boucher

slakter

The Butcher sells fish.

pharmacien

farmasøyt

That Pharmacist saved a person's life.

réceptionniste

resepsjonist

He is a Receptionist.

politicien

politiker

He wants to be a Politician.

guide touristique

tur guide

That Tour guide led us around Japan.

entrepreneur

entreprenør

He is an Entrepreneur.

danseuse de ballet

ballettdanser

She is training to be a Ballet dancer.

astronaute

astronaut

He is a great astronaut.

juge

dømme

That Judge is always fair.

avocat

advokat

The lawyer is serious.

la caissière

kasserer

She is a cashier at the market.

conducteur de taxi

drosjesjåfør

He is a fast Taxi driver.

plombier

rørlegger

That Plumber fixes toilets.

musicien

musiker

She wants to be a Musician like her teacher.

chef

chef

The chef makes fast food.

boulanger

baker

That baker is a bread.

artiste

kunstner

That Artist came from Italy.

acteur

skuespiller

That actor is famous.

barman

barkeeper

The Bartender works in a bar.

coiffeur

frisør

That girl is a Hairdresser.

évêques

bishops

He is a Bishop.

opticien

optiker

She went to an Optician.

fleuriste

florist

She is a great Florist.

écrivain

forfatter

He is a famous author.

comptable

regnskapsfører

My accountant is loyal.

du vin

vin

That wine tastes good.

café

kaffe

That coffee is bitter.

limonade

limonade

The lemonade is refreshing.

chocolat chaud

varm sjokolade

I drink hot chocolate every day.

milk-shake

milkshake

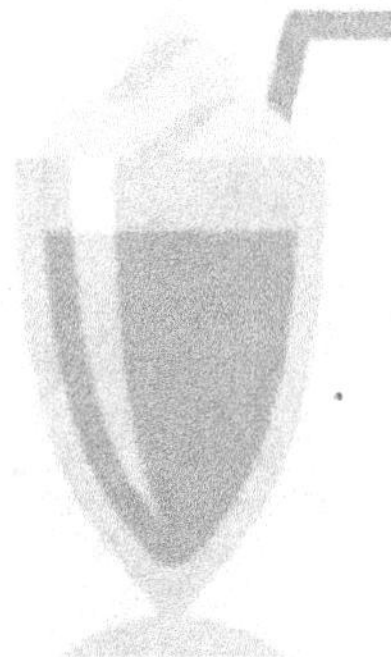

The milkshake has whipped cream.

eau

vann

The water is not cold.

thé

te

The tea is hot.

lait

melk

Milk is white.

bière

øl

The beer is foamy.

un soda

soda

The soda is fizzy.

smoothie

smoothie

The smoothie is a watermelon flavor.

milk-shake

milkshake

The milkshake has whipped cream.

lait de coco

kokosnøttmelk

The coconut milk is yummy.

du jus d'orange

appelsinjuice

The orange juice is made from oranges.

cacao

kakao

The cocoa is sweet.

fromage

ost

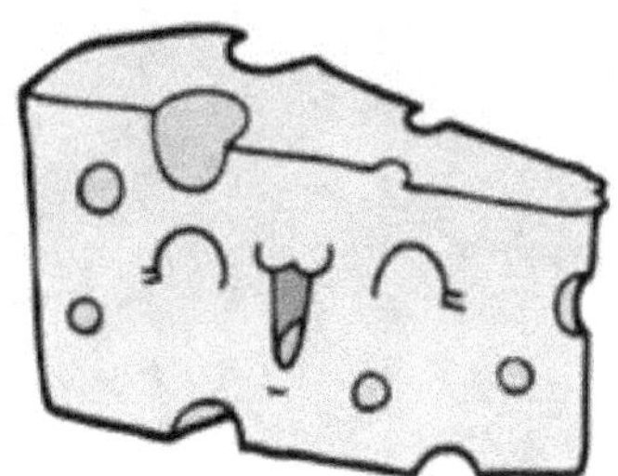

The cheese is creamy.

oeuf

egg

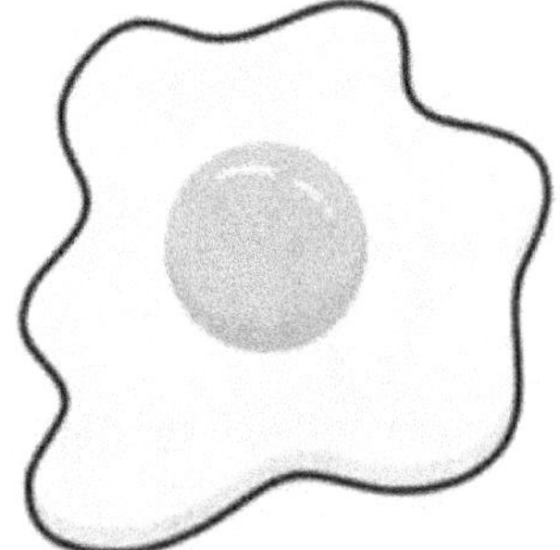

The egg is fried.

beurre

smør

The butter is put on bread.

margarine

margarin

Margarine looks like butter.

yaourt

yoghurt

That yogurt is popular.

cottage cheese

kesam

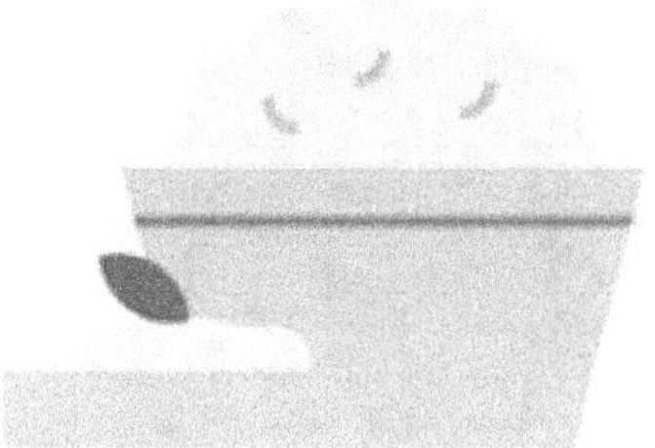

The cottage cheese is put on crackers.

crème glacée

iskrem

They have a triple scoop ice cream.

crème

krem

That is a lot of creams.

sandwich

smørbrød

That sandwich is healthy.

saucisse

pølse

Americans love sausages.

hamburger

hamburger

That hamburger looks happy.

hot-dog

pølse

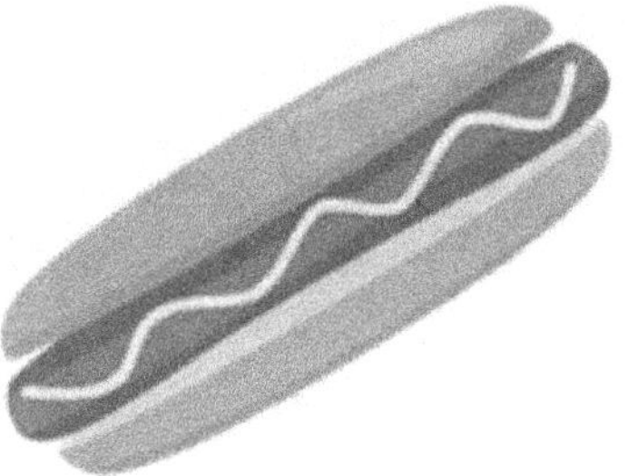

That hot dog has mustard on it.

pain

brød

That bread is saying hello.

pizza

pizza

That pizza is cheesy.

steak

biff

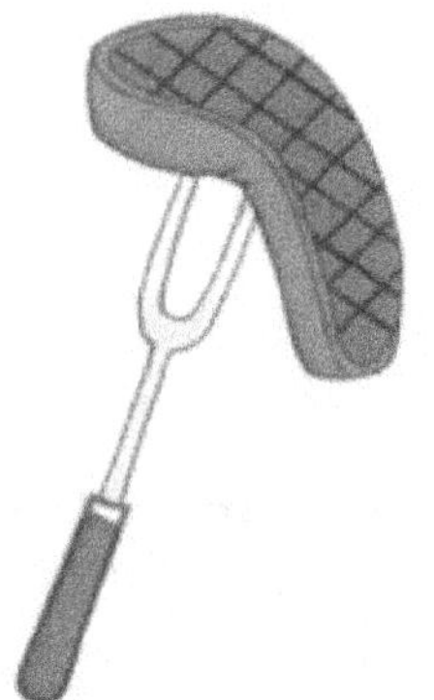

The steak was grilled.

poulet rôti

stekt kylling

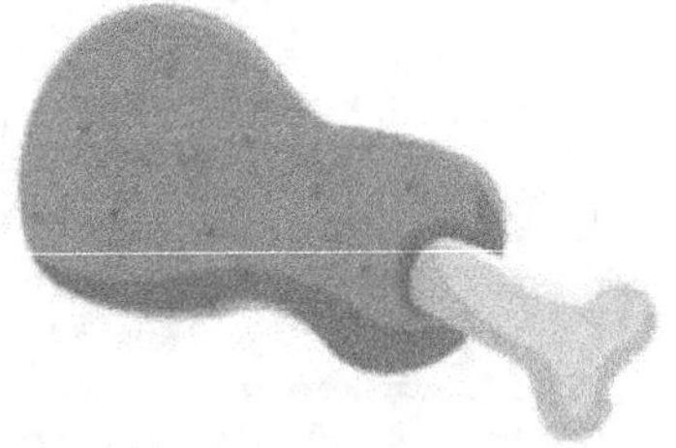

Roast Chicken is delicious.

poisson

fisk

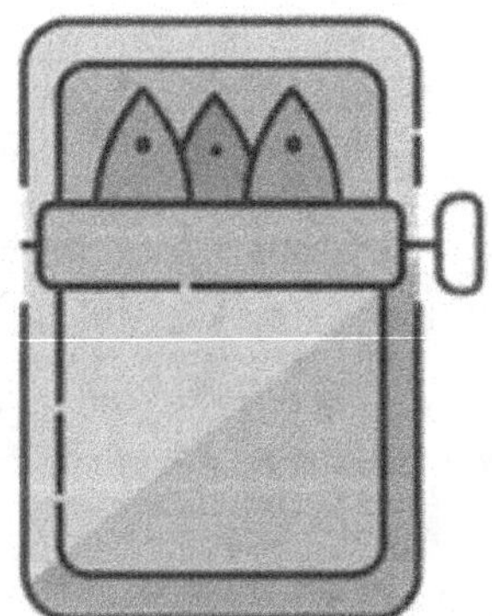

You can buy canned fish in the market.

fruit de mer

sjømat

Lobster is expensive seafood.

jambon

skinke

Ham can be put in sandwiches.

kebab

kebab

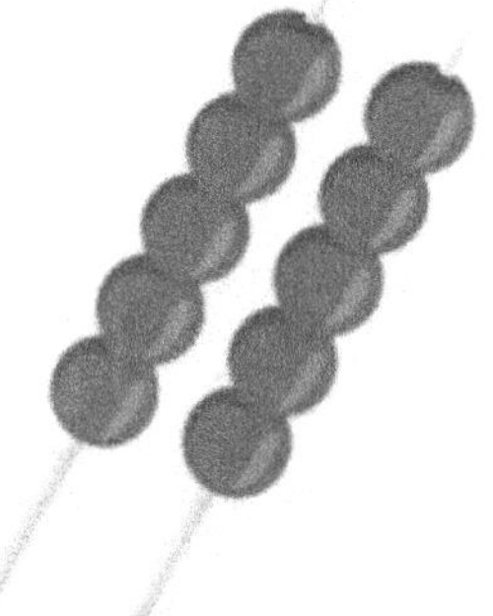

Kebab is a delicacy in America.

bacon

bacon

That bacon is smiling.

crème fraîche

rømme

You can dip your chips in sour cream.

vache

ku

Cows are black and white.

lapin

kanin

That rabbit is fun to play with.

canard

and

That duck is content.

crevette

reke

The shrimp has six legs.

porc

gris

That pig is pink and fat.

abeille

bie

The bee has a stinger.

chèvre

geit

That goat has a white horn.

crabe

krabbe

The crab has two big pincers.

cerf

hjort

That deer is sleeping.

dinde

tyrkia

The turkey has a giant tail.

colombe

due

That dove is carrying a plant.

mouton

sau

That sheep has fluffy wool.

poisson

fisk

That fish has colorful fins.

poulet

kylling

That chicken is waking everybody up.

cheval

hest

The horse has a red mane.

chaise

stol

That wing chair is yellow.

meuble tv

tv-benk

The TV stand can hold books.

canapé

sofa

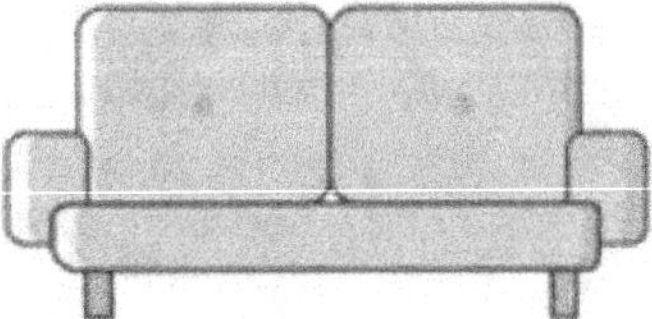

The sofa is comfortable to sit on.

coussins

puter

The cushion helps soften your seat.

téléphone

telefon

The telephone is ringing.

télévision

fjernsyn

That television is big.

haut-parleurs

høyttalere

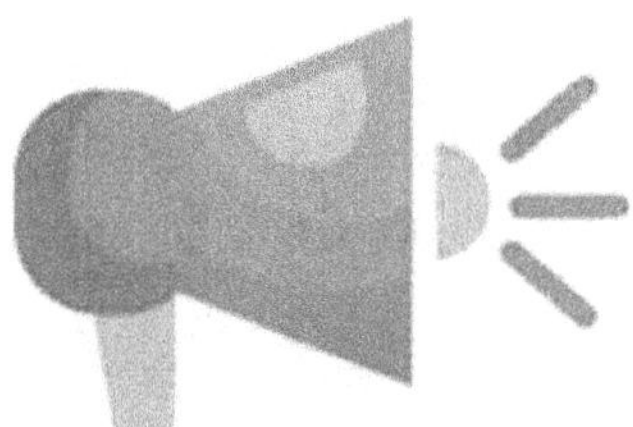

That speaker is used to increase the volume.

table d'appoint

sidebord

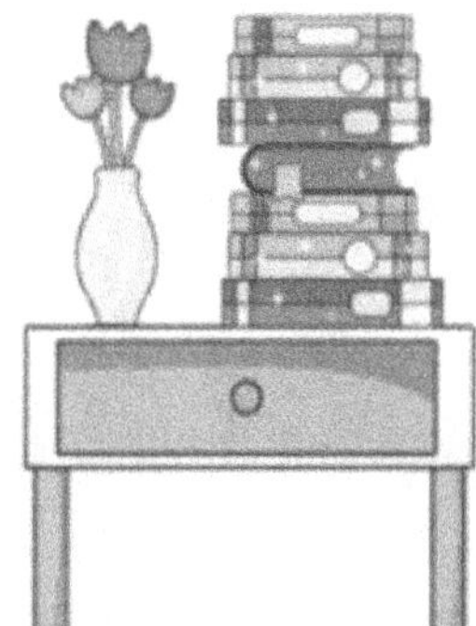

That end table is sparkling clean.

service à thé

tesett

That tea set is from China.

cheminée

peis

The fireplace makes me warm.

télécommandes

fjernkontroller

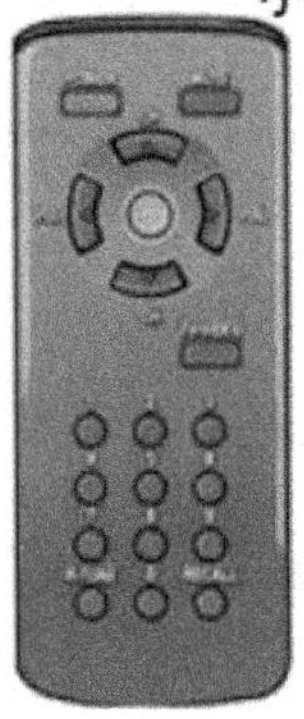

The remote has lots of buttons.

ventilateur électrique

elektrisk vifte

The fan is blowing wind.

lampadaire

gulv lampe

The floor lamp is very tall.

tapis

teppe

The carpet is soft and silky.

bureaux

skrivebord

The table is made of wood.

stores

blinds

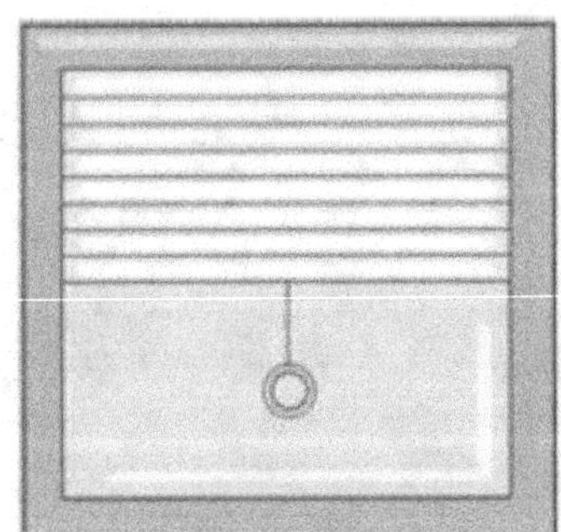

I will pull the blinds down.

rideaux

gardiner

She opened the curtains.

image

bilde

The picture is about the mountains and the sky.

vase

vase

The roses are all in a vase.

l'horloge

klokke

The alarm clock is beeping.

oreiller

pute

The pillow is pink and yellow.

cintre

lue henger

The hat stand has only one hat on it.

mettre la table

sminkebord

I have made up on my dressing table.

lampe de table

bordlampe

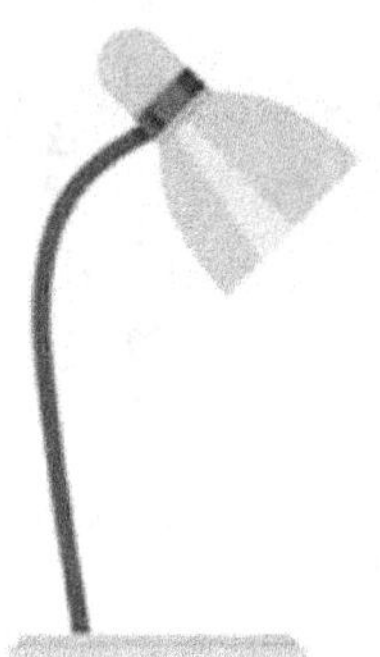

The table lamp will help me see in the dark.

miroir

speil

The mirror is very tall.

planche a repasser

strykebrett

Don't touch the ironing board, it's hot!

boîte avec tiroir

eske med skuff

You can keep your clothes in the hope chest.

table de chevet

nattbord

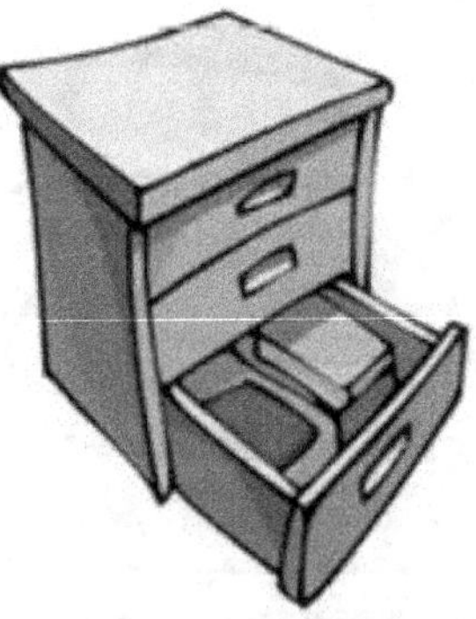

The nightstand has my lamp on it.

lit

seng

The bed is charming.

climatisation

klimaanlegg

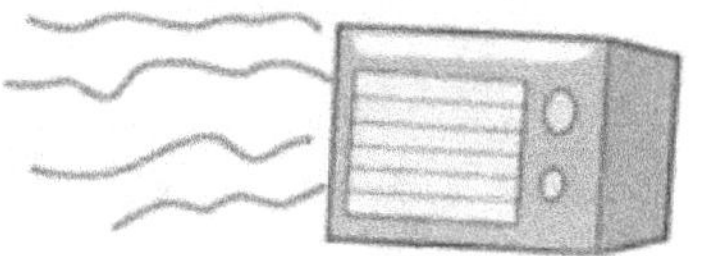

The air conditioner is cold.

cruche

mugge

The measuring jug has nothing inside.

dentifrice

tannkrem

The toothpaste is mint flavored.

brosse à dents

tannbørste

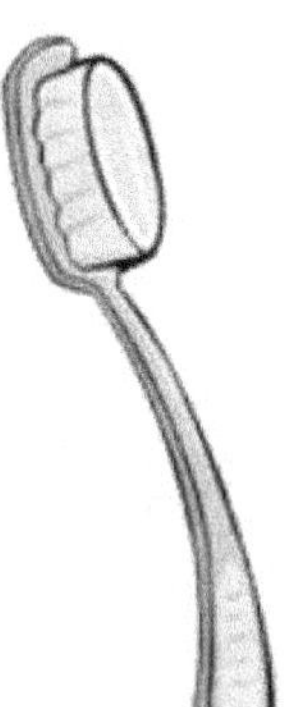

The toothbrush has toothpaste on it.

savon

såpe

The soap is very bubbly.

pince à linge

klesklype

The clothespin will clip my clothes.

cintre

hanger

The hanger is hanging my boots.

sèche-cheveux

hårføner

The hairdryer will blow my hair.

shampooing

sjampo

The shampoo is used to clean your hair.

bulle

boble

The bubbles are very fun to play in.

brosse

børste

She is brushing her hair with the brush.

papier toilette

toalettpapir

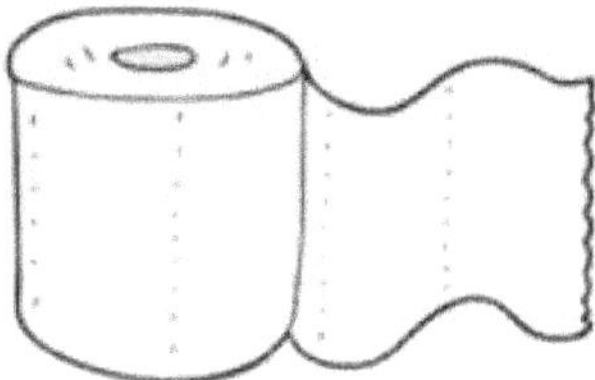

The toilet paper is used to dry your hands.

serviette

håndkle

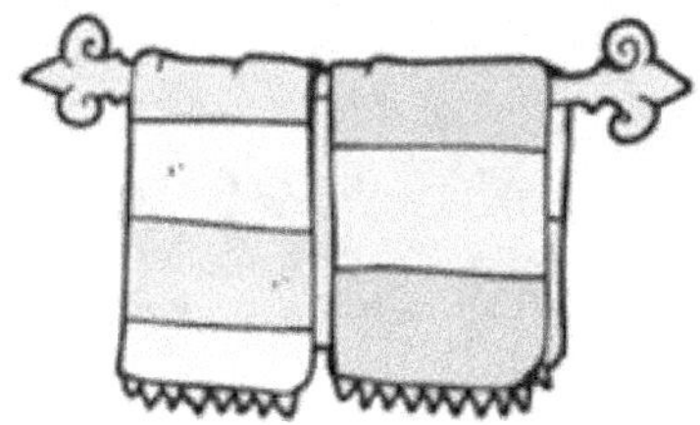

We have two towels on the rack.

corde à linge

klessnor

My shirt is hanging on the clothesline.

douche

dusj

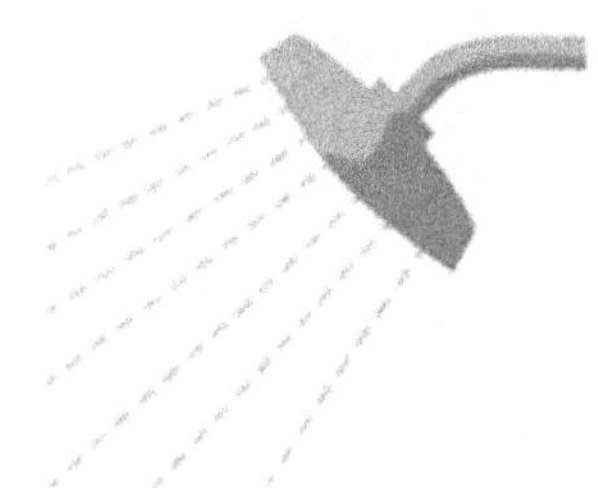

The shower is spraying water.

baignoire

badekar

The bathtub is comfortable.

lessive

vaskemiddel

The laundry detergent is used with the washing machine.

seau

bøtte

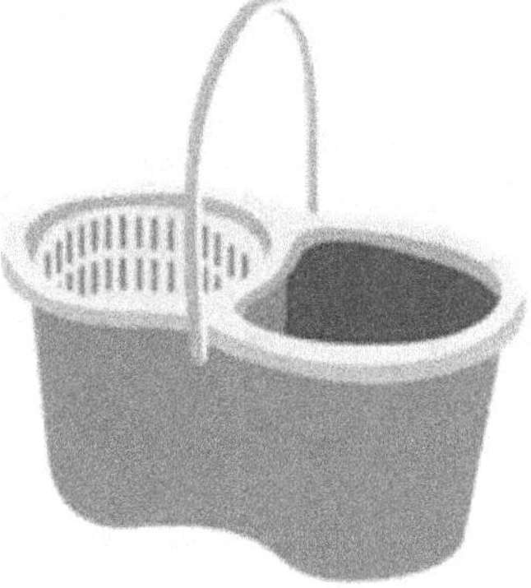

Can you help me fill up the bucket?

vadrouilles

mops

The mop is used for mopping the floor.

savon liquide

flytende såpe

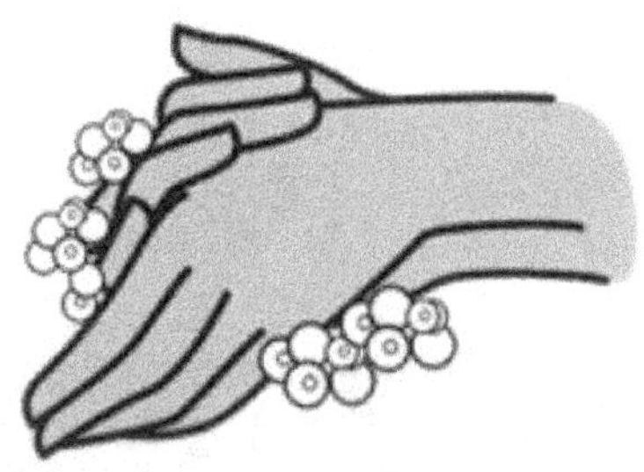

I use soapy water to wash my hands.

lessive en poudre

vaskepulver

I will scoop up the washing powder.

sac poubelle

søppelsekk

The trash bag is full of trash.

poubelle

søppelbøtte

You have only to put recylcle trash in the trash can.

les puits

vasker

You should wash your hands in the sink.

cuvette des toilettes

doskål

She let her bunny use the toilet.

machine à laver

vaskemaskin

The washing machine wash your clothes.

panier à linge

skittentøyskurv

She is putting all the clothes into the laundry basket.

le rasoir

barberhøvel

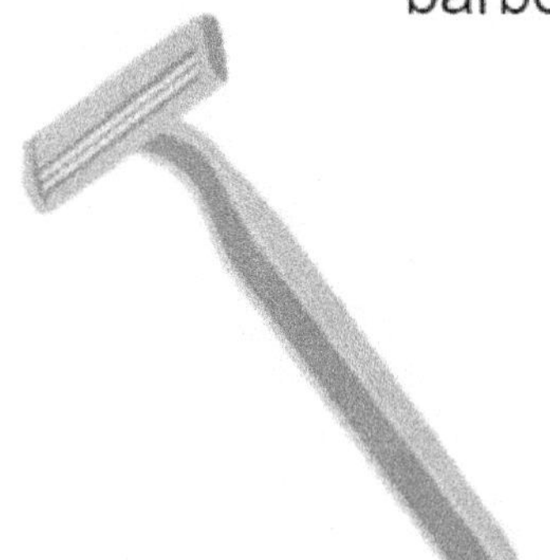

He uses the razor to shave his beard.

rasoir électrique

elektrisk barbermaskin

The electric razor works faster than the normal one.

crème à raser

barberkrem

The shaving cream is fluffy.

bain de bouche

munnvann

The mouthwash smells very lovely.

coton-tige

bomullsdott

Q-tip can be used for many things.

brosse à cheveux

hårbørste

She brushes her hair with her hairbrush.

peigne

kam

Her dad will comb her hair for her.

nettoyant

cleanser

Put the cap back on the cleanser bottle.

échelle

scale

You can measure things on the scale.

papier de soie

tørkepapir

The tissue is on the counter.

jouets de bain

badeleker

The little duck is a bath toy.

robinet

kran

The faucet is broken.

miroir

speil

He is looking in the mirror.

tapis de bain

baderomsteppe

The bath mat is purple and yellow.